William G. Morrice

WE JOY IN GOD

Foreword by William Barclay

London
SPCK

First published 1977
SPCK
Holy Trinity Church
Marylebone Road
London NW1 4DU

© William G. Morrice 1977

Quotations from the New English Bible, second edition © 1970,
are by permission of Oxford and Cambridge University Presses.

Printed in Great Britain by
Bocardo & Church Army Press Limited
Cowley, Oxford

ISBN 0 281 02967 9

*We also joy in God through
our Lord Jesus Christ*

Romans 5.11

Authorized Version

CONTENTS

CONTENTS

FOREWORD

It gives me real pleasure to write this foreword to Dr Morrice's book *We Joy in God*. The purpose of this book is to examine the 'Why?' and the 'How?' of Christian joy. Dr Morrice does this in a most comprehensive way. The teaching of the New Testament is examined, the light that the great doctrines throw on Christian joy is also examined, and the results of the examinations are lucidly and wisely set down.

This is a timely book. It would be a timely book under any circumstances because, to our misfortune, we don't specially connect Christians with joy. We tend rather to connect Christianity with having to do the things we don't want to do and having to stop doing the things we do want to do. We forget that, as Dr W.R. Maltby once said, Jesus promised his disciples three things. He promised they would be in constant trouble, completely fearless, and absurdly happy. The joy of the Christian faith has been demonstrated rather by people like the Pentecostalists than by orthodox Christians, and it may well be that it is for that reason that the Pentecostal Church is the fastest growing Church in Christendom. In point of fact, the Church of Scotland — to take only one example — has for the last ten years been losing an average of 25,000 members per year, and it may well be that the joy of the Pentecostalists is the reason for their growth and the comparative joylessness of orthodox Christianity is the reason for its decline.

This book, therefore, will do Christianity a real service if it turns the thoughts of Christians to joy and shows the way to it and the sources of it.

This is a good book, thoroughly biblically based and thoroughly and wisely discussed, and we cannot but wish it every success when it is issued to the public.

WILLIAM BARCLAY

INTRODUCTION

Two recent entertainments in London — the pop musical *Godspell* and the film *Jesus Christ Superstar* — emphasize in their own way the concept of joy that lies at the very heart of Christianity. Taken along with the modern revival of interest in charismatic gifts, in particular 'speaking with tongues', these 'happenings' have focused attention on aspects of Christianity that are less traditional than ordinary services of worship. We may well ask how much of all this is a true expression of the mind and message of Jesus.

In contrast to these modern phenomena, most of which are taking place outside orthodox Church circles, the attitude of many people towards Christianity can be summed up in Swinburne's words about Jesus: 'Thou hast conquered, O pale Galilean; the world has grown grey from Thy breath' ('Hymn to Proserpine'). It would appear that, in the minds of the masses, the joy and the colour have been taken out of religion. This may account for the fact that many denominations report year by year a steady fall in the number of Church members in spite of an increase in the population. On the other hand, the Pentecostal Churches have grown so rapidly during the past half-century that they have been referred to as a 'third force' in world Christianity.

It may be that orthodox Christians are partly to

blame for this state of affairs by being joyless people. Perhaps there is nothing to which we have such need to be recalled as the quality of joy; for

> . . . men have such need of joy!
> But joy whose grounds are true;
> And joy that should all hearts employ
> As when the past was new.[1]

The purpose of this book is to examine the 'why?' and the 'how?' of Christian joy. This concept is firmly based in the New Testament. It is founded upon important Christian doctrines such as the Fatherhood of God, the incarnation, the resurrection of Jesus Christ, and the Holy Spirit. This being so, how can this idea be worked out in practical terms? Francis of Assisi expressed the matter in a picturesque way: 'Let us leave sadness to the devil and his angels. As for us, what can we be but rejoicing and glad?'

I take this opportunity of expressing my thanks to Professor A.M. Hunter for starting me off on the quest for joy in the New Testament and for his help to me throughout the years; to Professor William Barclay for encouraging me at various stages in the quest and for so graciously agreeing to contribute a foreword; and to my wife, who has patiently and joyfully endured the long process of my research into the meaning of Christian joy.

Unless otherwise indicated, I have followed the New English Bible for biblical quotations. Occasionally, I have used the following translations: Authorized Version (AV); Revised Standard Version (RSV); The Translator's New Testament (TT); William Barclay (WmB).

1

GOD AS FATHER

The most important name we human beings have for God is that of 'Father'. This was the new revelation given to us through Jesus Christ. Yet it was not a new title for God. Greeks and Romans often referred to the gods as the fathers of the human race. Homer, for example, looked upon Zeus as 'the great father', 'the father of gods and of men'. Yet physical paternity was normally involved. The Hebrews lifted the idea out of the natural level and transplanted it into the spiritual.

In his teaching about God as Father, Jesus was drawing to a certain extent upon common Jewish doctrine. His enemies had no quarrel with him about his general teaching on this subject, but they did object to his specific claim to have equality with God by calling God his own Father (John 5.18; cf. John 8.41).

Much is said about God as Father in the Old Testament. Sometimes he is spoken of as Father in the sense of Creator (Isa. 64.8; Mal. 2.10); but more often the title signifies a spiritual relationship between God and the people of Israel. Not only so; but we hear of God promising to be as a father to individuals — to kings such as Solomon (2 Sam. 7.14) and David (Ps. 89.26) and even to others within the nation, 'all who fear him' (Ps. 103.13). Hosea came to regard God both as Husband and as Father. Through these two deep relationships of human life, the prophet expressed his conception of the love of God for the nation.

3

Such teaching about God as Father — already present in Judaism before the time of Christ — was taken over into Christianity from the very start. Yet in the process of being taken over, it was adapted and developed. The idea was so deepened that God came to be recognized more completely as the Father of individuals as well as of the community, as the Father of all mankind rather than of Israelites exclusively or in particular.

This development can be partially paralleled in rabbinic Judaism of the time of Jesus. By the first century A.D., the Jews had less hesitation about applying the name of Father to God. It may be that Jesus borrowed this title for God from the popular usage of his time. Nevertheless, Jesus went very much further than any of his fellow Jews would have gone when he dared to call God by the familiar word, *Abba* — the Aramaic equivalent of our 'Daddy'. This was the intimate way in which Jesus addressed God in prayer.

In his teaching about God, Jesus often referred to God as 'Father' — 'my Father' or 'your Father' or 'the Father' (especially in the fourth Gospel) or 'Father' (in the vocative case). When speaking to his disciples, Jesus could say, 'my Father and your Father' (John 20.17), but never did he say, 'our Father' (that is, 'our' = 'my' + 'your'), although in the Lord's Prayer he told them to say, 'Our Father . . .'. His filial relationship with God was on a different plane from theirs. Nevertheless, the Gospels show us that Jesus frequently and naturally called God 'Father'.

Thus, one of the main purposes of the coming of Jesus into this world was to reveal God to men as their heavenly Father. In his work of preaching and healing, Jesus showed that God is interested in individuals, whatever their social standing. In the Upper Room, he said to his disciples: 'Anyone who has seen me has seen the Father' (John 14.9). Earlier on in his ministry, when the seventy (or seventy-two) had returned from their mission of evangelism, Jesus rejoiced in the fact that the revelation of God as Father had been given to ordinary men and women and that they had learned to trust in him as their heavenly Father. Such faith could bring new joy into their lives. Jesus gave thanks to God for the prospect of seeing this brought to pass through the successful issue of the missionary campaign in Galilee (Matt. 11.25; Luke 10.21).

Providential and Individual Care

In the Sermon on the Mount, Jesus insisted that the cure for worry lay in utter trust in God as Father (Matt. 6.25-34; cf. Luke 12.22-31). Anxious care concerning food, drink, and clothing is senseless, he maintained. He pointed to the birds of the air as examples of reliance upon God's providence and to the lilies of the field as models of disregard for dress. God knows that we cannot do without these material things, and he will provide them for our use. Free from anxious worries about bodily needs, we can rejoice in our heavenly Father's providential care over us.

But is it not too much to expect that God should be interested in every man and woman in the world? In face of the big things of nature and on account of the fact that there are so many of us, it seems impossible that every single person should be of infinite worth in the eyes of God. By insisting upon the Fatherhood of God, Jesus taught that the divine love is as all-embracing of mankind as is a human father's concern for his own children. In order to emphasize this truth, Jesus mentioned the sparrows, two of which were sold for a penny; but not one could fall to the ground without the knowledge of God (Matt. 10.29). Since God cared in this way for the cheapest life in the market, he cared still more for human beings, who were infinitely more valuable. In Luke's account (Luke 12.6), Jesus declares that five sparrows were sold for two pennies. One would appear to have been thrown into the bargain as an extra of no account; but not even that extra sparrow is forgotten before God. If God loves the sparrows and cares for them like that, how much more must he love and care for men, who are so much more precious to him!

In the fourth Gospel, the image used is that of the sheep given into the keeping of Jesus by his Father. Since God is greater than all, 'no one can snatch them out of the Father's care' (John 10.29). The knowledge and assurance of such individual care lavished upon Christians by their heavenly Father can give them a new sense of joy in the face of the chances and changes of mortal life. Whatever happens to us, we are safe in the Father's hands. Nothing can separate us from the love of God in Christ Jesus our Lord.

This trust in God's providential and individual care produces such a relationship with the heavenly Father that we can be led into new and broader visions of prayer. God is more willing to bestow blessings upon individuals than they are to pray for them. God is more ready to help than is a human father. We Christians are therefore encouraged to ask for things from God (Matt. 7.11; Luke 11.13; Phil. 4.6). The model prayer given by Jesus to his disciples also put the Fatherhood of God into the very forefront of their thinking and practice in prayer. 'This is how you should pray: "Our Father in heaven . . ." ' (Matt. 6.9).

Life after Death

The assurance of joy in the life after death rests upon the conviction of the unconquerable love of God as Father. Jesus taught that doing the will of the Father earned the reward of entrance into 'the kingdom of heaven' (Matt. 7.21).

In the farewell discourses, Jesus assured his disciples that there were many dwelling-places in his Father's house (John 14.2) and that he was going away to prepare a place for them. He himself saw in his imminent departure to be with the Father a cause for joy in the disciples rather than sadness, and he chided them upon their sorrow (John 14.28). Not even death could break his fellowship with the Father, and his last words to his followers were spoken in order that they too might share his joy in God as Father (John 15.11). He prayed that they might have the fulfilment of that communion in the next world by sharing in his glory (John 17.24). The Father's providential care both of Jesus and of his disciples thus extended beyond the narrow confines of this world of space and time.

Redemptive Activity

God is also seen as Father in his redemptive activity. The very heart of the Christian message is found in the fourth evangelist's summary statement about God's love shown forth in the gift of his only Son and about God's purpose of eternal life for all who have faith in him (John 3.16). God the Father was active in redemption through Jesus Christ in order to restore men and women into fellowship with himself (2 Cor. 5.19). The filial relationship had been broken by means of human sin, and it could only be restored after the repentance of sinners and their forgiveness by God.

7

Jesus conceived of his own mission as a call to repentance (Mark 1.15). His proclamation of the divine forgiveness was closely associated with his conception of the fatherly love of God for all his children. One of the six petitions in the Lord's Prayer clearly links the recognition of God as Father with the human cry for forgiveness: 'Our Father . . . forgive us . . .' (Matt. 6.9,12).

Jesus told three parables to emphasize God's joyful and loving forgiveness of sinners. We find them all together in chapter fifteen of Luke's Gospel. The shepherd searches for his lost sheep until he has found it; then he summons his friends and neighbours to celebrate the recovery. Luke thus emphasizes the gladness in the heart of God at the restoration of one lost soul (Luke 15.4-7). As the woman who has lost one of ten coins cannot remain content with only nine, so God misses even one unrepentant sinner. Her persevering care in searching for her missing treasure reminds us of God's untiring redemptive activity on behalf of men and women. Her overflowing joy on finding the lost coin emphasizes the exuberant joy of God over one sinner who repents (Luke 15.8-10). The climax of the chapter comes in the parable of the prodigal son (Luke 15.11-32): having repented of his sins, the younger son was forgiven by his father on his return home. His restoration to the family circle is described in the father's orders to the servants concerning the best robe, the ring, the shoes for his feet, and the killing and eating of the fatted calf. These all showed the foolish boy that he had been forgiven by his father and that he had been restored to his proper place in the household. The attitude of the scribes and the Pharisees to sinners is depicted in the behaviour of the elder son, who was annoyed with the festivities held to welcome his brother back home. The last word in the parable, however, is given to the father. It is a word that expresses love for both his sons.

It has often been pointed out that the redemptive activity of God as Father described in these three parables goes far beyond anything found in rabbinical Judaism. Although synagogues welcomed repentant sinners, they did not go out of their way to bring them in. The initiative was largely left to sinners. Jesus, on the other hand, sought out the despised members of the Jewish community — the tax-collectors and the sinners — and consorted with them, because of his larger vision of God as Father. He conceived of his own mission as the Messiah sent by the Father in terms of the redemption and the salvation of such people as Zacchaeus, the tax-collector at Jericho, for 'the Son of Man has come to seek and save what is lost' (Luke 19.10).

The Joy of Forgiveness

In modern theology, it is usual to identify forgiveness with reconciliation and to regard justification as the Pauline version of forgiveness. Vincent Taylor has shown that, in the New Testament, forgiveness covers only the remission of sins and is distinct from, though a necessary preliminary to, reconciliation or restoration to fellowship with God.[1]

The joy of forgiveness comes before us in the story of the paralytic who was brought to Jesus by his friends. Jesus saw in him the deep depression caused by the overwhelming burden of sin and, with a kindly word of encouragement, gave to him a new freedom (Matt. 9.2). In the parable of the prodigal son, on the other hand, both forgiveness and reconciliation are present. The act of forgiveness came when the repentant younger son was yet at a distance. His father had been looking for him and went out to meet him, flung his arms round him and kissed him (Luke 15.20). Full reconciliation was possible only in the father's house when the returned prodigal had been restored to his filial position and was enjoying the banquet prepared by his father's servants.

While it is of minor importance to distinguish clearly between the two terms in the context of this parable, the distinction is vital to an understanding of the work of Christ upon the cross. Jesus did not die merely in order that we might be forgiven, and almost nowhere in the Gospels does he connect forgiveness with his death. There is however an apparent exception to this in Matthew 26.28; but the words 'for the forgiveness of sins' have been added by Matthew to the words of Jesus as found in Mark 14.24 — perhaps under the influence of Jeremiah 31.31-4. Jesus died rather in order that we should be restored into full fellowship with the Father. In the death of Christ, God was reconciling the world to himself in a way that was not possible apart from the supreme sacrifice made upon the cross (2 Cor. 5.19). As a result, we 'joy in God through our Lord Jesus, through whom we have now received reconciliation' (Rom. 5.11 — my own translation). It was for this reason that Paul refused to boast of anything but the cross of Jesus Christ (Gal. 6.14).

The joy of fellowship with the Father has thus been opened up for Jew and Gentile alike through the death of Christ (Eph. 2.18). Yet it cannot be maintained by selfishly hoarding it as a private possession, but it must be shared in order to be preserved in its fullness. The writer of the Johannine letters knew this. His purpose in writing was to lead his readers into the divine fellowship and thereby to complete his own joy (1 John 1.3f.). Fellowship with the Father could, however, be broken and, as a matter of fact, was continually being broken, since we all sin (1 John 1.8). John links up the thought of God as Father with his proclamation of the forgiveness of sins (1 John 1.9). Furthermore, Christ is our advocate with the Father, and through him we can be restored to the divine fellowship (1 John 2.1f.).

This assurance of the forgiveness of sins and of reconciliation with the Father effected by Jesus Christ helped to bring about the new atmosphere of joy among the first circle of believers. The Fatherhood of God became for Christians 'not a mere article in a creed or just a title for God, but a burning conviction, a spiritual experience which gave new meaning and value to life, and brought new peace and joy to human hearts'.[2] The whole of the New Testament was written out of this background.

The transforming power of this teaching about God as Father can be seen in such a chapter as Romans 8, which has been described as 'a splendid fugue on the theme of the Fatherhood of God'.[3] God's fatherly care of us in providence and in redemption is summed up by Paul in magnificent words: 'As we know, he co-operates for good with those who love God and are called according to his purpose' (Rom. 8.28). The climax comes with his shout of joyful conviction that there is nothing in heaven or on earth that can separate us from the love of God — a love that has been revealed to us in and through the teaching of Jesus Christ about God as Father.

2

GOD IN CHRIST

Christianity is not merely a religion of the Fatherhood of God and the brotherhood of man, as some nineteenth-century liberal theologians would have had us believe. It is firmly rooted in historical events, chief of which are the incarnation, the crucifixion, and the resurrection. In fact, Christianity is the only religion that actually depends entirely upon history, since it proclaims divine redemption from within history through God incarnate as a human being in Jesus Christ.[1]

There is, of course, no doctrine of the incarnation in the Old Testament. Yet the roots of such an idea can be traced there. For centuries before the birth of Jesus, the Jews had been anticipating the coming of a deliverer. Out of the midst of successive political oppressions by great powers, the Israelites looked to God for help and matched their afflictions with hopes of deliverance. In the Old Testament, God himself is usually thought of as the author of the fulfilment of the nationalistic hopes of salvation, but a human agent was by no means ruled out. This human agent, who came later to be regarded as 'Messiah' (that is, 'Anointed One' — for which the Greek is *christos* = 'Christ'), was represented in various idealized personages who were familiar and respected in Judaism: the priest (Ps. 110.4; cf. Heb. 5.6), the prophet (Deut. 18. 15; Mal. 3.1, 4.5), and the king. The most important of these personages was the ideal Davidic king, who towers so high above the other figures and so dominates the scene of Jewish speculations about the future that the name 'Messiah' later came to be used as a technical term for the whole hope of Israel.

The figure of this individual agent emerged first of all with the prophet Isaiah who, amid the national disasters of his day, prophesied national deliverance and prosperity under a divinely appointed king. The exultant prophecy of Isaiah 9.2-7 comes to a climax with the report of the birth of such a king, 'in purpose wonderful, in battle God-like, Father for all time, Prince of Peace'. Again, in Isaiah 11.1, we are told that 'a shoot shall grow from the stock of Jesse, and a branch shall spring from his roots'. The prophet Micah foretold the town in which the coming deliverer would be born: 'Bethlehem in Ephrathah' (Mic. 5.2). Both Jeremiah and Ezekiel tell of this future king of the house of David (Jer. 23.5, Ezek. 34.23, 37.24). These passages, however, could mean little more than that the Davidic dynasty would be continued in the time of the restoration. In this period, there was no fixed doctrine of a Messiah, only material from which such a doctrine could later be drawn.

In Haggai 2.23 and in Zechariah 3.8 and 6.12, the hope of the coming deliverer is connected with the name of Zerubbabel, leader of one of the groups who returned from the Babylonian exile (Ezra 2.2, Neh. 7.7). In Zechariah 9.9, there is a wonderful picture of a victorious king, 'humble and mounted on an ass' — a prophecy made use of by Jesus in his triumphal entry into Jerusalem on Palm Sunday (Matt. 21.5).

It should be carefully noted that in none of these passages does the term 'Messiah' actually occur. As a matter of fact, the word never appears in its technical sense in the Old Testament, but is so used for the first time in history in the Pseudepigrapha, books written under assumed names in the inter-testamental period. In one of the 'Parables of Enoch' (probably written between 94 and 64 B.C.), we are told that the kings of the earth 'have denied the Lord of Spirits and his Anointed One' (Enoch 48.10). The future kingdoms of the world, symbolized by seven metal mountains, show the Messiah's might by melting before him (Enoch 52.4). If, as Dalman argues,[2] these passages must be rejected as later interpolations, the first occurrences of 'the Messiah' as a technical term would be in the Psalms of Solomon. These eighteen psalms were written in Hebrew in the middle of the first century B.C. (between 70 and 40) by Pharisees in opposition to the worldly, non-Davidic monarchy and illegitimate priesthood of the ruling Hasmonean king, Aristobulus. The Messianic hope is seen especially in Psalm 17, where there is the promise that God will 'raise up to them their king, the son of David. . . . All shall be holy and their king the anointed of the Lord.' This great king will be 'pure from sin'. 'Nations shall come from the ends of the earth to see his glory.' Yet this king is to be merely the vice-gerent of God, for the psalm closes with the words: 'The Lord himself is our king for ever and ever.'

All these ideas — the priest, the prophet, and the king — belong together in that they involve a conception of the Messiah in human terms. Gradually there emerged alongside them the figure of a pre-existent divine Messiah, a heavenly being. In the Book of Daniel (second century B.C.), there is related a vision of 'one like a son of man coming with the clouds of heaven; he approached the Ancient of Years [i.e., God pictured as a very old man] and was presented to him.

14

Sovereignty and glory and kingly power were given to him, so that all people and nations of every language should serve him. . . '(Dan. 7.13f.). This title of 'the Son of Man' is given messianic significance in the Parables of Enoch. He is Judge of the world, Revealer of all things, Champion and Ruler of the Righteous (Enoch 46.1ff., 48.1ff.).

Thus the figure of 'the Messiah' emerged in Judaism in the first century B.C. although the conception had its roots in the idealized personages of the priest, the prophet, and the king as portrayed in Old Testament prophecy and in Daniel's vision of the son of man. Gradually, all the nationalistic hopes of the Jews came to be centred in 'the Messiah' — 'the Anointed One'. Yet the Jews did not speculate on the metaphysical status of the Messiah. They were vague in their ideas about his nature — whether human or angelic or divine. Nevertheless, they were convinced that his function was the inauguration of the kingdom of God by his action from within history.

The Incarnation

In such ways as these, the ground was being prepared for the great historical event of the incarnation. 'When the term was completed, God sent his own Son, born of a woman, born under the law' (Gal. 4.4). When we remember the eager anticipation for the coming of the Messiah, we can understand the joy with which the birth of Jesus was greeted by the circle of pious people who did not belong to the parties of the Pharisees or the Sadducees, but who, nevertheless, 'watched and waited for the restoration of Israel' (Luke 2.25). The joy of Mary herself at the promise of the coming fulfilment in the birth of her son appears in the

15

'Magnificat' (Luke 1.46-55). In this song, Mary rejoices in God her Saviour because of his mercy both to herself personally and to the nation of Israel. The same note of gladness over the birth of a 'deliverer' — the Messiah, the Lord (Luke 2.11) — was struck in the message of the angel to the shepherds who were keeping watch over their flocks through the night: 'Do not be afraid; I have good news for you: there is great joy coming to the whole people' (Luke 2.10). When the young child was brought to the Temple by his parents, he received a welcome from Simeon and Anna, two devout people who frequented the holy place (Luke 2.25-38). By relating these incidents connected with the birth and early childhood of Jesus, Luke shows the joy with which the incarnation was greeted by this small group of pious Jews, which included people like Mary and Joseph, as well as Elizabeth and Zechariah, the parents of John the Baptist.

But it was not only the Jews who had yearnings for redemption. The ancient world at the time of the incarnation was one that was sorely in need of a Saviour. This need showed itself in the emergence of various religious movements within the pagan world itself. Chief of these were Stoicism, Epicureanism, and the Mystery Religions. Since a characteristic note in such systems was the longing for redemption, the Gentile world also was being prepared for the coming of Jesus Christ.

Surprisingly, it is Matthew, the Jewish Christian evangelist, who, in his story of the visit of the wise men or astrologers from the east, symbolizes the joy of the non-Jewish world at the incarnation. By following the new star they had discovered in the heavens, they were eventually led to Bethlehem. When they saw the star above the sacred spot, 'they were overjoyed'

(Matt. 2.10), since they realized that their quest was at an end. In that little town of Bethlehem the hopes of Jews and Gentiles met together at the incarnation.

Jesus often emphasized the note of joyful fulfilment in his teaching. In his first sermon at Nazareth, he took as his text words from the Book of Isaiah where the ideal prophet is pictured as one who would be anointed by the Spirit to preach a gospel of liberation and healing, comfort and joy (Isa. 61.1f.; Luke 4.18f.). Jesus told the astonished people in the synagogue at Nazareth that this text had come true in their very hearing (Luke 4.21). Again, in 'the beatitude of privilege', the disciples were congratulated upon their good fortune in experiencing the blessings of the messianic age (Luke 10.23; cf. Matt. 13.16). Previous generations had desired to share in these blessings, but their hopes had been disappointed. Similarly, in the fourth Gospel, Jesus is reported to have spoken of Abraham's joy at the vision that was granted to him of the incarnation either in anticipation or in heaven (John 8.56).

New Testament Doctrine

Although there is no systematic doctrine of the incarnation as such in the New Testament, but only the material from which such a doctrine was later formed, each of the writers was convinced that God was in Christ. In him, what may be described as 'the absolute', 'the ultimate', or 'the supra-historical' had entered into the field of human history. The various books have different ways of trying to express this truth.

Mark represents Jesus in such a way that a doctrine of his pre-existence is ultimately implied. He is both 'Son of God' and 'Son of Man' — a being of super-

17

natural origin and dignity whose humanity is nevertheless evident in his emotional make-up and in the limitations of his knowledge.

The supernatural position of Jesus as 'Son of God' is explained in part by the doctrine of the virgin birth, which is unmistakably taught by both Matthew and Luke, but nowhere else in the New Testament is there certain reference to it.[3] The idea is not essential to the divinity of Christ nor to the doctrine of the incarnation. We could still believe that God was in Christ even if he had a human father as well as a human mother. Yet the virgin birth can be seen as an attempt to emphasize the truth of the incarnation, even though Luke at least by no means depends on it for his Christology. In fact, if it is true, as Vincent Taylor argues,[4] that Luke 1.34f. was a later interpolation made by Luke himself when he came across the tradition after the first draft of his Gospel had been written, this would help to prove that in the first instance such a doctrine was not felt to be essential to the Christian message. It may have been incorporated into the text later on the ground that the idea of a virgin birth made 'a fitting preface to the life that was crowned by resurrection from the dead'.[5] An additional argument in support of this contention is that the doctrine of the virgin birth had no part in the earliest Christian preaching as seen in the Acts of the Apostles and in the Pauline Letters.

In the fourth Gospel, Jesus is the eternal Son of God — the Word of God in human form. He became incarnate of his own free will in order that those who believed in him might have eternal life and receive power to become children of God. The fact of the incarnation is also emphasized in the First Letter of John in opposition to the docetic views that were

18

arising towards the end of the first century A.D. Only those who believe that Jesus is the Christ, the Son of God, and that he has truly come in human form are true Christians and can know that they have eternal life.

Although the cross and the resurrection formed the central pivots of the Apostle Paul's faith and theology, he was also convinced of the truth that has come to be formulated in the doctrine of the incarnation. 'When the term was completed, God sent his own Son' (Gal. 4.4). . . 'in a form like that of our own sinful nature, and as a sacrifice for sin' (Rom. 8.3). The earthly life of Jesus Christ, who had 'divine nature from the first', is held out to Christians as an example of true humility in the christological hymn in Philippians 2.5-11. In 2 Corinthians, Paul used the fact of the incarnation to give extra strength to his special appeal for the Jerusalem collection. He urged that 'each person should give as he has decided for himself; there should be no reluctance, no sense of compulsion; God loves a cheerful giver' (2 Cor. 9.7). He pointed to the divine example set in such giving: not only does God provide men with 'ample means' (2 Cor. 9.8), but he has given to us a 'gift beyond words' in Jesus Christ (2 Cor. 9.15).

The author of the Letter to the Hebrews also realized the importance of the doctrine of the incarnation and understood how central it was to the idea of the finality of the Christian revelation (Heb. 1.1f.).

The rest of the writers of the New Testament had similar views with regard to the great event that had taken place in the coming of Jesus Christ into the world, and they sought to express their convicitons in their own ways. One and all, they realized that something unique had happened, and they strained human language in their efforts to describe what was ultimately inexpressible, since nothing like it had ever taken place before. God had become man, the divine had entered into the arena of human history and had been working from within history to redeem mankind.

Uniqueness of the Doctrine

The uniqueness of this event is underlined by Augustine in his *Confessions*. He tells us how, in his reading of a Latin translation of some neo-Platonic writings, he had come across the doctrine of the divinity of the eternal Word of God, but that there were two passages in St John's Prologue that he could not trace there. There was no parallel to the idea that 'he came to his own, and his own would not receive him. But to all who did receive him, to those who have yielded him their allegiance, he gave the right to become children of God.' Then Augustine continues: 'Again I read there that "God the Word was born not of flesh, nor of blood, nor of the will of man, nor of the will of the flesh, but of God". But that "the Word was made flesh and dwelt among us", I read not there.'

Christianity, therefore, owes its uniqueness in part to the doctrine of the incarnation. In fact, no other religion is so materialistic and so historical at its very roots. The various New Testament writers all tried to make this clear. The fact that God had entered into the world on the first Christmas Day made all the difference to their attitude to the world and to life both here and hereafter.

Thus, the joy of the Christmas season is no superficial emotion. It is not merely the spirit of good will and brotherly kindness, but goes deep down into the depths of Christian faith and is firmly rooted within the pages of the New Testament.

Before we can celebrate Christmas aright, we have to go in spirit once again to Bethlehem with the shepherds and 'see this thing that happened' (Luke 2.15) when God entered human life in the baby lying in a manger. Only when we have done that will it be truly said of us, as it was of the converted Scrooge at the close of Dickens' 'Christmas Carol', 'that he knew how to keep Christmas well, if any man alive possessed the knowledge'.

3

THE RISEN CHRIST

Belief in the risen and ascended Christ plays an important part both in the New Testament and in Christian theology. In fact, the doctrine of the resurrection of Jesus from the dead is the keystone in Christianity. The subtraction of this central dogma of the faith would mean the collapse of the Christian Church. Nor could it be excised from the pages of the New Testament without destroying the whole. Everything depends upon this great act of God in raising Jesus Christ from the dead. If it had not happened, we could have had nothing vital upon which to base our Christian faith. Because Jesus was raised again and is alive for evermore, we celebrate not only the festival of Easter but also Sunday as our day of Christian worship.

Surprisingly, therefore, little is said about resurrection in the Old Testament. For centuries, the Jews seem to have been content with teaching about Sheol, the place of the departed, where life was hardly worth living. The one unambiguous reference to resurrection is in the last of the thirty-nine books to be written (Dan. 12.2). There we read that many will awake to everlasting life, but some to shame and everlasting contempt.

How, then, could the early Church say that Jesus was raised to life on the third day according to the Scriptures (1 Cor. 15.4)? It is possible that 'according to the Scriptures' should be taken closely with 'on the third day' and not with the previous phrase, 'that he was raised to life'. There are vague references in the Old Testament to something happening 'on the third day' (Hos. 6.2; 2 Kings 20.5).

In the apocalyptic literature of the inter-testamental period (that is, the time between the writing of the last book of the Old Testament and the writing of the earliest book of the New Testament), the idea of resurrection is found. It is said, for example, that the righteous will be raised to take part in the messianic kingdom, though the wicked will either remain in Sheol or be transferred to Gehenna, the place of torment (1 Enoch 25.4ff., 22.13).

Nevertheless, in Judaism at the time of Christ there was no firmly fixed doctrine of resurrection. It is even surprising that Jesus himself said little about it in his teaching. It is true that in debate with the Sadducees Jesus based belief in the resurrection both on the Old Testament Scriptures and on the power of God (Mark 12.24). Yet he also transferred the resurrection from the last day to the moment of death by saying to Martha, 'I am the resurrection and I am life' (John 11.25).

The fact that this doctrine is largely absent from the teaching of Jesus as well as from the Old Testament and from Judaism focuses our attention on his own resurrection. Only this event — whatever it was and however it came about — could have brought the doctrine from the circumference of religious thought to its very centre.

Within the New Testament, there are two different lines of tradition regarding the resurrection of Jesus Christ. The earliest tradition, found, for example, in 1 Corinthians 15, is that of Easter appearances of the risen Lord to his disciples and apostles. There is also the later tradition regarding the discovery of the empty tomb. In the fourth Gospel, both these traditions have been fused together.

Post-Resurrection Appearances

In one of his letters to Christians at Corinth about A.D. 54 or 55 (1 Cor. 15.3-8), Paul gives us the earliest written record of the Easter story. This depends on tradition that goes back to within six years of the crucifixion and resurrection.[1]

In this important passage, there are four clauses introduced by 'that':

(1) The first clause — 'that Christ died for our sins according to the Scriptures' — proclaims not only the fact of the death of Christ but also its theological significance. It was 'for our sins' that Jesus died on the cross.

(2) The second clause — 'that he was buried' — makes no explicit reference to the story of the empty tomb. Nowhere does Paul clearly record this discovery.

(3) The third clause — 'that he was raised to life on the third day according to the Scriptures' — implies not simply the revivification of a corpse but the complete transformation into a new existence — the kind of resurrection anticipated in the apocalyptic literature, especially in Daniel and in Enoch.

(4) The fourth clause falls into three parts, each of which contains the verb 'he appeared' (the Greek verb is *ophthe* = 'he was seen'). This may mean that Paul had three informants, Peter, one of the five hundred, and James:

and that *he appeared* to Cephas and then to the

24

twelve; then *he appeared* to over five hundred of our brothers at once, most of whom are still alive, though some have died; then *he appeared* to James and then to all the apostles.*

To this list of official witnesses to the resurrection appearances, Paul adds himself: 'In the end *he appeared* even to me . . . '

The fourfold 'he appeared' has been defined as meaning that Jesus 'came out of the sphere of eternity and invisibility and was made manifest by God'.[2]

This passage, as we have already noted, is the earliest written account that we possess of the Easter story. It says nothing at all about the empty tomb. Instead, everything depends upon the appearances of the risen Christ to his disciples and apostles. In those very early days, therefore, faith in the risen Lord was based not upon the empty tomb but upon their own personal encounters with their risen Lord.[3]

The Evidence of the Empty Tomb

Of course, even though Paul says nothing at all about the empty tomb, this does not necessarily mean that he knew nothing about it. Nor does it mean that the reports about the empty tomb are not reliable. Even the Jews appear to have agreed with Christians that the tomb was empty; for Matthew records their attempt to explain it away (Matt. 28.13). The fourth Gospel tells how Mary of Magdala jumped to the conclusion that 'they' (perhaps she meant by this the enemies of Jesus) had taken the body away (John 20. 13). Any such theory, however, that involves the stealing or hiding away of the body of Jesus seems incredible. If the Romans or the Jews had been responsible for the theft, why did they not produce

*My own translation.   25

the body later in order to refute the preaching of the apostles? They did not because they could not. If the disciples had been responsible, they could not have used the empty tomb as evidence for the resurrection. In all four Gospels, we find reports about the empty tomb.

In Mark, the first of the four Gospels to be published, probably at Rome about A.D. 65, the resurrection narrative is found in chapter 16.1-8, where, in our earliest and best Greek manuscripts, Mark's Gospel comes to an abrupt end. Verse 7 shows that Mark knew about appearances of the risen Christ in Galilee. Verse 6 implies that Jesus was no longer on earth and that he had already been translated into heavenly existence: 'He has risen; he is not here.' The empty tomb is given as evidence of this truth. If this 'material' evidence was not communicated to the disciples till later, as the second part of verse 8 suggests, then it follows that they received it 'not as the origin and cause of their Easter faith, but as a vehicle for the proclamation of the Easter faith which they already held as a result of the appearances'.[4]

Matthew received through Mark's Gospel, which he used as one of his chief written sources, the traditions about the empty tomb. In his narrative in chapter 28. 1-20, however, he has also added much material that is secondary — for example, the stories about the earthquake, the appearance of an angel, the rolling away of the stone. It seems that Matthew conceived of the resurrection in physical terms. It almost looks as if the rolling away of the stone was necessary in order to facilitate the resurrection from the tomb (Matt. 28.2). The women were able to clasp his feet (Matt. 28.9); nevertheless, he is also a divine being whom they worship. But to the account of the empty

26

tomb, which he received from Mark, Matthew has added not only secondary features. He has also appended a spiritual appearance of the risen Christ in Galilee (Matt. 28.16-20).

There is a different account of the Easter events in Luke's Gospel. Leaving aside minor discrepancies — such as the number of women at the tomb and the number of men (or angels) who appeared to them — we find in Luke the story of the walk to Emmaus (Luke 24.13-33) and the appearance to the eleven in Jerusalem (Luke 24.36-49). This is followed by the ascension at Bethany (Luke 24.50f.) and the return of the disciples to Jerusalem with great joy (Luke 24.52). Unlike Matthew, Luke leaves no room for any appearance in Galilee; but he does emphasize the empty tomb (Luke 24.12,24). In fact, Luke's shift away from Jesus' resurrection appearances to the empty tomb as the primary explanation for the disciples' Easter faith is a tendency that is even more marked in John 20.[5]

In the fourth Gospel, the two traditions about the resurrection of Jesus have been skilfully combined. In John 20.2-10, there is the account of how Mary ran to tell the disciples about the empty tomb and of how two of them went to verify her report. Verse 8 indicates that, according to the fourth evangelist — probably relying upon the memory of 'the other disciple' — belief in the resurrection came, not as the result of any appearances of the risen Christ, but rather — first and foremost — on the evidence of the empty tomb. 'The other disciple' (probably John, 'the beloved disciple') 'saw and believed.' The whole of this section (John 20.2-10), however, could well be an insertion by the evangelist into the story of the appearance of the risen Christ to Mary of Magdala. If this is so, the two traditions have been carefully woven together in the fourth Gospel.

The Reality of the Resurrection

Up to recent years, New Testament scholars have insisted upon the historicity of the empty tomb as an essential part of the documentary evidence for the resurrection of Jesus Christ. This is no longer the case. Professor Marxsen, for example, suggests that 'the statement "Jesus is risen" must on no account be interpreted as if the tomb had been empty'.[6] What is clear from our study of the two-fold tradition in the New Testament is that in the earliest form of the tradition (found especially in 1 Cor. 15.3-8) faith in the risen Christ rested upon his appearances to his disciples after his resurrection. Only later was the account of the discovery of the empty tomb brought forward as evidence. Wherever it is mentioned, there is a tendency to consider the resurrection as being physical.

More important than the question of the historicity of the empty tomb is that of the reality of the resurrection itself. What kind of event was the resurrection of Jesus Christ from the dead? It was an historical event in the sense that something really happened. Yet it was something that happened outside the history of this world of space and time. Since it took place between this world and the next — between time and eternity — it has been called 'meta-historical'.[7] As such it left only a negative mark within history: 'He is not here' (Mark 16.6). Yet the risen Christ is always with us and can be apprehended by the eyes of faith. Our Christian faith depends, therefore, not so much on factual details of a historical nature (such as the account of the empty tomb), but on our risen and ascended Lord, who 'makes himself present and visible to those to whom he chooses to reveal himself'.[8] This is the emphasis found in the fourth Gospel's account of how Thomas came to believe in the resurrection. Jesus said to him: 'Because you have seen me you have found faith. Happy are they who never saw me and yet have found faith' (John 20.29).

The Preaching of the Early Church

From the very start, the doctrine of the resurrection of Christ held a central place in the preaching of the early Christian Church. There was only one gospel as proclaimed by the first apostles, and in it the passion and the resurrection of Christ had the pre-eminent place. These events had occurred 'in accordance with the Scriptures'. Jesus was the Messiah shadowed forth in the Old Testament prophets. After going about doing good and healing the sick in body and in mind, he was innocently delivered up to be crucified. But God raised him from the dead and exalted him to his right hand in glory. Such was the *kerygma* — the pattern of the earliest preaching as it emerges from the sermons in the Acts of the Apostles and from various passages in the Pauline Letters.[9] It centred round the mighty act of God for the deliverance of the world through the death and the resurrection from the dead of his only Son. Wherever this *kerygma* was preached, it brought new hope to people and turned many away from the disillusionment of ancient heathenism to the Christian faith. The Christian Church was thus founded upon the Easter event and the fact of the risen Christ.

The centrality of the doctrine of the resurrection in the thought of the Apostle Paul is apparent from his letters. He could no more contemplate Christian preaching without this event than he could envisage a world without the sun. We have already noted how, at

29

the beginning of 1 Corinthians 15, Paul gives the earliest written record of Easter appearances of the risen Christ to disciples and apostles. A few verses later, he uses a *reductio ad absurdum* argument in order to show that the Christian faith and Christian experience in their entirety presuppose the resurrection of Christ. After showing that if the resurrection were not a reality there would be no Christian gospel, no Christian faith, no forgiveness of sins, no hope of life after death (1 Cor. 15.14-18), he declares: 'But the truth is, Christ was raised to life — the firstfruits of the harvest of the dead' (1 Cor. 15.20).

Thus, the doctrine of the risen Christ, which was a vital part of the apostolic *kerygma*, was the presupposition of all Paul's preaching and of the theology lying behind it. It made a big difference to his whole idea of God. The God in whom he now believed was the Father who had raised Jesus Christ from the dead (Gal. 1.1; Rom. 4.24; cf. 1 Pet. 1.21). This was the vindication of the whole life, ministry, and passion of our Lord, and the seal set upon all that Jesus had taught about the nature and the character of God the Father. So Paul linked together indissolubly the cross and the resurrection as mutually dependent and complementary events within the mighty act of God. The cross was meaningless apart from the resurrection, just as the resurrection could not have taken place without the death of Christ. While Paul gloried in the cross of Jesus Christ, he did so in the light of Easter, for Jesus 'died on the cross in weakness, but he lives by the power of God' (2 Cor. 13.4).

The resurrection of Christ also involves other doctrines: the ascension and the exaltation of the risen Christ. Paul and the other early Christians believed not only that Jesus had been raised from the dead by God

and that he was alive for evermore. They were convinced that he reigned supreme as King of kings and
Lord of lords (Rev. 17.14, 19.16) and that he continually interceded for Christians before the throne of
God. We also believe, as they did, in Jesus Christ, 'who
died, and more than that, was raised from the dead —
who is at God's right hand, and indeed pleads our
cause' (Rom. 8.34).

The Letter to the Hebrews represents an area of
Christian thought where the doctrine of the resurrection was merged into that of the exaltation. Its
unknown author regarded Christ as our great High
Priest, who entered into heaven and 'is always living
to plead on our behalf' (Heb. 7.25).

Victory over Sin

Having considered the centrality of the resurrection of
Christ in the New Testament, we shall now try to
assess its significance for Christians today. This doctrine is much more than an illustration of human
survival after death. 'It is a victory uniquely won, and
won in order that mankind may be enabled to share in
Christ's resurrection. It does for us what we cannot
do for ourselves.'[10]

What, then, is the nature of this victory won on
our behalf by Jesus Christ? It is, for one thing, victory
over sin. Because Jesus Christ died and rose again from
the dead, the Christian lives in a new sphere in which
he can overcome sin and temptation in the power
supplied by Christ. In other words, Christian ethics
are resurrection ethics. By his union with Christ, the
Christian believer shares in his victory over sin. 'Were
you not raised to life with Christ? Then aspire to the
realm above, where Christ is' (Col. 3.1). It is God who
is the Author of this new life; for, being 'rich in mercy'

31

and 'for the great love he bore us', he 'brought us to life with Christ even when we were dead in our sins' (Eph. 2.4ff.).

All this implies that the resurrection of Jesus Christ has something vital to say to each of us for our life here in the present world. It assures us of the immense possibilities inherent in human flesh, weak though it all too often is. The grace of Christ is sufficient for us, since his power — the power of his own victory over sin — is made perfect in our weakness (2 Cor. 12.9). Divine grace is thus available for us at the very point where our own strength is at its lowest ebb, and we can overcome temptations in the power supplied to us by God throught the death and the resurrection of Jesus Christ (1 Cor. 15.57).

The author of 1 Peter touches on this in the course of an exhortation to holy living. He reminds us that 'it was no perishable stuff, like gold or silver, that bought your freedom. . . The price was paid in precious blood, as it were of a lamb without mark or blemish — the blood of Christ' (1 Pet. 1.18ff.). It is the cross in the light of the resurrection that is in view here (see 1 Pet. 1.21). Thus set free from sin, Christians can live a new life of peace with God and fellowship with the risen Christ.

Victory over Death

The victory won on our behalf by Christ is also victory over death. Christians have been delivered from the fear of death which lay heavily upon the ancient pagan world (cf. Heb. 2.15). They have been 'raised to life with Christ' (Col. 3.1), so that death remains 'only as an enemy defeated and spoiled of his power. It is no longer the last word. It has become a road along which those who are Christ's may pass to a fuller sharing of his life.'[11] So the Apostle Paul could always be of good courage, since he knew that to be away from the body was to be at home with the Lord (2 Cor. 5.8). The risen Christ is 'the firstfruits of the harvest of the dead' (1 Cor. 15.20). The body of the Christian after death is to be like that of the risen Lord — glorious, incorruptible, immortal (1 Cor. 15.35-57).

The First Letter of Peter opens with an outburst of praise for the resurrection of Jesus Christ, whereby Christians have been given 'new birth into a living hope' (1 Pet. 1.3). They have been set free from death by the blood of Jesus Christ as the Hebrews had been set free from the land of Egypt by the Passover lamb (1 Pet. 1.18f.).

Thus the exultant message of the New Testament is that death has been conquered by one who through his own death has overcome the grave and opened to men the gate of everlasting life. ' "O death, where is your victory? O death, where is your sting?" . . . God be praised, he gives us the victory through our Lord Jesus Christ' (1 Cor. 15.55,57).

4

THE HOLY SPIRIT

From the beginning of history, men have been aware of some mysterious power which entered into their lives from time to time and caused them to do extraordinary things. At the outset of all religions, we can trace the idea of the Spirit in its rudimentary phase, but it came to its fullness within the field of Hebrew and Christian traditions. The doctrine of the Holy Spirit emerged as an explanation of something that was profoundly felt — by Hebrew prophets, by the early Christian apostles, as well as by revivalists and mystics of more modern times. In the early Old Testament literature, the Spirit was simply the power whereby a man was capable of marvellous actions (see, e.g., Judg. 6.34, 14.6). Gradually, the idea was brought under the influence of the moral and ethical requirements of the religion of Yahweh, the Holy One of Israel.

Old Testament thought never entirely escaped from the notion — which we encounter again in the New Testament and in the charismatic movement of the present day — that the activity of the Spirit is sudden and spasmodic instead of being the more or less permanent possession of religious men and women. The eighth-century prophets,[1] however, came far on the way towards a better understanding of the work of the Spirit. Isaiah, for example, realized that men are helpless 'until a spirit from on high is lavished upon us' (Isa. 32.15). Of ourselves, we are weak and require strength from God. This same prophet declared that the Spirit would be given in its fullness to the coming descendant of David and that the Spirit would rest upon him as his enduring possession (Isa. 11.2). A sixth-century prophet felt that the Spirit of the Lord rested upon him because he had been anointed by God (Isa. 61.1), just as Jesus later felt when he quoted Isaiah's words in the course of his sermon in the synagogue at Nazareth (Luke 4.18). Yet another prophet, early in the fourth century B.C., realized that not only chosen leaders but all the people would share in the outpoured Spirit of God — so much, so that young people would prophesy and old men would dream dreams (Joel 2.28; cf. Acts 2.17).

In respect of this doctrine as in other cases also, the fulfilment of Old Testament ideas is found in the New Testament. When the early Christians became aware of the strange new force working within them and recalled its appearance in Jesus in the days of his earthly life, they described it in terms of the Old Testament doctrine of the Spirit. References to the Holy Spirit are, therefore, very frequent in the New Testament, appearing, in fact, in every book except 2 and 3 John and Philemon.

Jesus and the Holy Spirit

The Synoptic Gospels make it clear that the life of Jesus was inspired by the Holy Spirit from beginning to end. Matthew and Luke both open with narratives which trace the relation of Jesus to the Spirit back to his conception and birth (Matt. 1.18,20; Luke 1.35). All three synoptists tell how the Spirit like a dove descended upon Jesus at his baptism in the River Jordan, remaining with him as his constant possession.

Although they do not mention the Spirit at every step in his ministry, presumably because they considered him to be in full possession of the Spirit continually, they believed that this divine power accompanied all his work and words.

It is in Luke's Gospel *par excellence* that we find prominence given to the Holy Spirit. Since it is also the Gospel of joy, this indicates the close association between the two ideas. In his Gospel, Luke emphasizes the work of the Holy Spirit in the life and ministry of Jesus, while in the Acts of the Apostles he stresses the work of the Holy Spirit in the life of the Church during the thirty years after the resurrection of Christ. As far as Luke was concerned, therefore, the Holy Spirit presided over the beginnings of Christianity from the birth of Jesus to the establishment of the gospel at the heart of the Roman Empire.

Furthermore, Luke alone of the three synoptic evangelists explicitly states the connection between the Holy Spirit and joy. John the Baptist's 'leaping for joy' before his birth (Luke 1.41,44) is mentioned in close association with the fact that Elizabeth was filled with the Holy Spirit (Luke 1.41) and in explicit fulfilment of the prophecy to his father that he would be filled with the Holy Spirit from his birth (Luke 1.15). The exultant joy of the unborn babe over the visit of the mother-to-be of the Messiah is paralleled by that of Jesus himself on the return of the seventy missionaries. Luke describes the violent outburst of emotion experienced by Jesus on account of the fresh proof given to him of the Father's purpose and method of revealing himself to ordinary men and women. The exultant joy of Jesus was divinely inspired (Luke 10.21).

If we had only this passage to go by, we would have to infer that Luke represents a return to the older conception of the Spirit as acting spasmodically upon people and as giving rise to ecstatic speech or extraordinary and unusual action. Elsewhere, however, the evangelist makes it clear that Jesus was in possession of the Holy Spirit at all times. He would have attributed to the divine power working within Jesus his joyful attitude to life as a whole. Along with Mark and Matthew, Luke believed that it was in the power of the Spirit that Jesus carried on his ministry in its entirety. This is made particularly evident when Luke quotes the text of Jesus' sermon at Nazareth: 'The Spirit of the Lord is upon me because he has anointed me. . . '(Luke 4.18; cf. Isa. 61.1). This prophecy had been fulfilled in Jesus Christ. His work and words as God's Messiah were all due to the influence of the Holy Spirit upon him.

Christians and the Holy Spirit

The experience of the Holy Spirit, however, was no preserve of Jesus alone. The fourth Gospel makes it clear that Jesus gave the Holy Spirit to his disciples when he met them after his resurrection (John 20.22). This was the climax of the fellowship that they had enjoyed with him during his earthly ministry. It was also the fulfilment of the promise he had given to them to send them the Paraclete. In five different sayings during the farewell discourse, Jesus had promised the Holy Spirit to them as a perpetual presence (John 14.15-17), a perpetual teacher (John 14.25-6), a perpetual witness to himself (John 15.26-7), a perpetual convicter of wrong (John 16.7-11), and as a perpetual adviser or revealer of the truth (John 16.12-15). By giving a masculine name to the Spirit (*parakletos*) in addition to the neuter abstract noun (*pneuma* = breath, wind, spirit), John helped not only to personalize the Holy Spirit but also to prepare the way for the doctrine of the Trinity. The Paraclete is the Spirit of truth given to Christians by the Father.

In the sequel to his Gospel, Luke also shows how the early Christians were conscious of the same divine power within themselves as had been within their Master. Before his exaltation, the risen Christ had promised to send the Spirit to his disciples so that they might be armed with power from above (Luke 24.49; Acts 1.5-8). According to Luke, this promise was fulfilled on the Day of Pentecost, when the waiting Christians were all filled with the Holy Spirit (Acts 2.4). Luke has a confused and confusing description of the events of that day. In particular, he refers to the fact that the crowd who gathered round the apostles were amazed because each one heard the apostles speaking in his own language. This does not seem to be the 'glossolalia' or 'speaking with tongues' with which Paul had to deal in his Corinthian correspondence (1 Cor. 12.10,28; 14.26f.). Nevertheless, whatever it was that actually happened on the Day of Pentecost was expressly attributed by Peter to the outpouring of God's Spirit in fulfilment of Joel's prophecy (Joel 2.28).

The whole progress of the Christian mission in ever-widening circles — from Jerusalem to Judaea, then to Samaria, then to the ends of the earth (Acts 1.8) — was governed by this divine power working within the apostles. In fact, the Acts of the Apostles might well be called 'the Acts of the Holy Spirit' since at almost every step in the advance of the Church the work of the Spirit is explicitly acknowledged. There is one occasion on which the Holy Spirit is linked with the joy experienced by Gentiles on hearing the gospel of salvation (Acts 13.48). This was in complete contrast to the Jews in that city of Pisidian Antioch. They were filled with jealousy on account of Paul's success (Acts 13.45). Luke considered that the joy of the Christians was closely associated with the fact that they were in possession of the Holy Spirit. Further than that he did not go: he never worked out fully the precise relationship between the two concepts, though he implied that their joy was inspired by the Holy Spirit as in the case of Jesus himself (Luke 10.21). As Professor Hunter has put it, 'Joy is a dominant characteristic of these Spirit-filled men of the primitive church in Acts.'[2]

Paul and the Holy Spirit

Paul refers to the Holy Spirit nearly 120 times in his letters. This was, therefore, a central theme in the gospel as he understood it. 'One might as well try to explain Paul's Christianity without the Spirit as modern civilisation without electricity.'[3]

Paul considered the Holy Spirit to be the permanent possession of the Christian believer. He made it the very test of Christian faith that a man should be endowed with the Spirit. Anyone who did not possess the Spirit of Christ was not a Christian in any real sense of the word (Rom. 8.9). A Christian is one who is spiritually alive, one who has a new outlook upon life, and one who can rejoice in hope (Rom. 12.11-12).

In what may be his earliest letter,[4] Paul drew up a list of nine virtues that were evidence of the presence of the Holy Spirit within the believer and described them as 'the fruit' or 'the harvest of the Spirit' (Gal. 5.22). It is important to notice that the first noun in this verse is in the singular (*karpos*) and not in the plural. These nine virtues form a unity, and together they describe the ideal Christian character created by God's Holy Spirit. They are 'the fruit [not fruits] of the Spirit', even though there is variety among them. Some apply to the inner life of the Christian — 'love, joy, peace'; others are seen in one's relationships with other people — 'patience, kindness, goodness'; others in one's personal character, shown in one's words and deeds — 'fidelity, gentleness, self-control'. The Holy Spirit bears fruit in every region of human life.[5] All nine qualities were pre-eminently visible in Jesus Christ himself, but they are also expected to be present in the life and character of every Christian believer as the harvest of the Holy Spirit who dwells in his heart. High in the list of Christian virtues comes 'joy', but greatest of all is 'love' — the love of God (*agape*) that 'has flooded our inmost heart through the Holy Spirit he has given us' (Rom. 5.5; cf. 1 Cor. 13.13). 'Joy' comes second and is followed by another virtue of the inner life, 'peace' — 'the peace of God, which is beyond our utmost understanding' and which can keep guard over our hearts and our thoughts (Phil. 4.7).

The joy of the Christian converts at Thessalonica is explicitly described as being inspired by the Holy Spirit (1 Thess. 1.6). In spite of the fact that they had had to suffer as Christians even before Paul had left their city (Acts 17.1-9) and had probably endured further persecutions once the apostle had moved on to Beroea, Athens, and Corinth, they could rejoice in their new-found faith on account of the presence with them of the Holy Spirit.

In his letter to Christians at Rome, Paul declares that the Holy Spirit helps him to realize God's love for him and assures him of future blessedness (Rom. 5.1-5).

His exultation is not dampened by sufferings, since he can still rejoice in his Christian hope. He is convinced that, in spite of all appearances, things cannot be against him in a world ruled by God.

Not only the assurance of God's love but also peace and joy are inspired by the Holy Spirit. These two inner virtues of the Christian life accompany justice or righteousness as the meaning of the kingdom of God, and all are due to the power of God's Spirit working within a Christian. Anyone who thus shows that he is a servant of Christ wins God's favour and the approval of men (Rom. 14.17f.). This reminds us of the saying of Jesus about setting our minds on God's kingdom and God's justice before everything else (Matt. 6.33). Instead of worrying about material things, we are counselled to cultivate the inner joy and peace that are inspired by the Holy Spirit and that give evidence of the presence of that Spirit in our hearts by righteous living.

As the main argument of the Letter to the Romans draws to a conclusion, Paul gathers together in a prayer the keynotes of the Christian life — hope, joy, peace, faith, and the power of the Holy Spirit (Rom. 15.13). The Holy Spirit is seen by Paul as the inspiration of Christian faith and Christian living, both in its inner aspects of love, joy, and peace and in its outward manifestations of righteousness and justice. The whole of the Christian life — not simply spasmodic 'spiritual gifts' — is governed by the Spirit.

Nevertheless, there are indications that Paul was not entirely satisfied with this doctrine of the Holy Spirit. Over and over again, he emphasizes the indwelling presence of the risen Christ. To this indwelling Christ, Paul attributes all the functions also attributed to the Holy Spirit. He had received the doctrine of the Holy

Spirit from his Christian predecessors, but he came to express the truth contained in it in terms of communion with his risen Lord. The presence of the Spirit for him was the spiritual presence of the Lord, and his most characteristic definition of a Christian was 'a man in Christ'. The phrases 'in Christ' and 'in the Lord' (both occur very frequently in the Pauline Letters) implied being both in communion with Christ and in the community of Christ, which is the Church. Both of these spheres of Christian experience, the personal and the corporate, are under the influence of the Holy Spirit. The fellowship of the Holy Spirit — that is, the fellowship that is created by the Spirit — is fellowship both with Christ and with his Church. It was in this spiritual fellowship with his risen Lord that Paul learned to rejoice.

Only once does Paul refer directly to 'joy in the Holy Spirit' (that is, 'joy inspired by the Holy Spirit' — Rom. 14.17). Instead, his most characteristic contribution to the Christian concept of joy can be summed up in another phrase, 'joy in the Lord' (Phil. 4.4). This Christian joy can be enjoyed in fellowship with Christ through the Holy Spirit. It is through the Spirit that Christ comes to the Christian believer and enables him to 'joy in God' .(Rom. 5.11 - AV).

The Holy Spirit Today

A study of the New Testament clearly indicates, therefore, that the Holy Spirit is an essential part of Christian experience and theology. Moreover, both inner joy and its outward expression are inspired by the Holy Spirit.

In the present-day charismatic movement, both these truths have been grasped, though only in part;

for in certain quarters the doctrine of the Holy Spirit is so tied up with 'speaking with tongues' that some would refuse to acknowledge other Christians as being truly inspired. They would maintain that those who do not possess this particular 'gift of the Spirit' do not possess the Holy Spirit at all. Glossolalia (that is, 'speaking with tongues') is regarded by some as being the only proof of true spirituality and real Christianity. What is the remedy to be in the present situation? I believe it should be threefold.

First, the Christian Church must not leave the doctrine of the Holy Spirit to the Pentecostalists, the Jesus Kids, or any other group of Christians. If the Church gives the impression that it does not even know whether or not there is a Holy Spirit (compare the recent converts whom Paul met at Ephesus in Acts 19.2), people will turn elsewhere for spiritual enlightenment. Yet surely all Christians believe in the power of the Holy Spirit even though glossolalia is not essential to every true believer. 'Speaking with tongues' was an aspect of early Church life that the Apostle Paul tried to play down in his correspondence with the Christians at Corinth, even though he admitted that he possessed the gift of ecstatic utterance himself (1 Cor. 14.18). In his Letter to the Galatians, he emphasized that the real evidence of the presence of the Holy Spirit in the life of a Christian is the manifestation of Christian virtues (Gal. 5.22).

Second, instruction in the faith should be offered in all humility to those who are over-emphasizing one particular doctrine to the neglect of other important Christian truths. This was what Aquila and Priscilla did with Apollos after they had heard him preaching in the synagogue at Ephesus (Acts 18.24-8). Apollos was a man of great spiritual fervour and of eloquent speech who had insufficient knowledge of Christian doctrine. After Aquila and Priscilla had expounded the new way to him in greater detail, his usefulness to the Church was greatly enhanced. A similar enrichment of the Christian Church could be the result today if those who have experienced one specific 'gift of the Spirit' could be instructed in all the doctrines of the Christian faith and remain within the fellowship of the 'one Holy Catholic and Apostolic Church' of Jesus Christ.

Third, before it can do either of these things, the Church must take a long, hard look at itself and at the image it is presenting to outsiders. We must ask ourselves: are we showing in our lives and in our public worship the joy of the Lord that is part of the nine-fold harvest of the Holy Spirit? This question has important implications for Christian life and worship.

5

WE SING FOR JOY

Joy in worship is very evident in the Old Testament, especially in the Book of Psalms, often referred to loosely as 'the hymn-book of the second temple'. In the psalter, we are told of the 'exultant shouts of praise, the clamour of the pilgrims' keeping festival (Ps. 42.4; cf. Isa. 30.29); and we hear the temple courts resounding with shouts of praise (Ps. 95.1). The author of Psalm 122 recalls the joy with which he received the invitation from his friends and neighbours to join them in their journey to Jerusalem to take part in one of the great festivals of the temple (Ps. 122.1).

These pilgrimages were occasions of thanksgiving to Yahweh on account of all that he had done for his people in delivering them from peril and danger of every kind. The Feast of Passover kept the people in joyful remembrance of the deliverance of their fore-fathers from the hands of the Egyptians. Similarly, the Feast of Purim was associated with the deliverance of the Jews under the Persians from the intrigues of Haman as shown in the Book of Esther.

Revitalized Christian Worship

With even greater reason than the ancient people of Israel, the new Israel could rejoice in God on account of what he had done for them in the fulfilment of his promises in the events centred round the incarnation, the resurrection, and the ascension of Jesus Christ. It is little wonder that the early Christian Church gave expression to its faith in revitalized worship. Those early Christians felt that the most astounding things had happened to them. Since 'a deep thankfulness and an irrepressible joy possessed them . . . their worship came from them much as its full-throated song comes from the bird — as the simple, spontaneous, over-flowing expression of an exuberant life that must of necessity have outlet'.[1]

Within the New Testament, it is Luke in particular who emphasizes this joy in worship. His Gospel closes, as it began, with worship in the temple; but the meaning of that worship has been transformed by the resurrection and the ascension of Christ. After their risen Master had parted from them outside Jerusalem, the disciples returned to the city 'with great joy, and spent all their time in the temple praising God' (Luke 24.52f.). They continued for the time being to attend the temple; but a new note had been given to their worship in the light of the marvellous events through which they had been living.

At the beginning of the Book of Acts, we find the early Christians still attending the temple, but in addition to this they met together in their homes, where they 'broke bread' and 'shared their meals with unaffected joy, as they praised God' (Acts 2.46f.). This breaking of bread (cf. Acts 2.42) may well be a reference to the Lord's Supper. In the earliest days of the Christian Church, this seems to have taken place within the setting of an actual meal. An essential characteristic of this meal was 'the exultant joy' mentioned here by Luke. This joy was inspired not so much by the remembrance of the last supper with Jesus in the upper room as by the remembrance of the post-resurrection meals shared by Jesus with his disciples.

46

These meals were looked upon as partial anticipations of the messianic meal promised at the last supper. The risen Lord had been recognized as he broke bread at the table of the two Emmaus disciples (Luke 24. 30,35) and, shortly afterwards, had eaten a piece of fish in the presence of the eleven and others in Jerusalem (Luke 24.43).

Thus, the joy of early Christian worship and, in particular, the rejoicing at the eucharistic meals of the early Church are to be explained not so much by reference to the Lord's Supper as such with its associations with the passion of Christ, but rather by reference to the resurrection and the joy of Easter. In fact, it was only because Jesus Christ did rise again from the dead that it was possible for those first Christians to rejoice at all. It was only natural that this Easter event should become the focal point round which the joy of Christian worship was centred.

The Lord's Day

The influence of the resurrection of Christ is to be seen in the fact that, from the very beginning, the first day of the week held a special significance for Christians as being the day on which Jesus Christ rose from the dead. It came to be known as 'the Lord's day'. Each Sunday was an Easter festival and as such a day of joy.

The emergence of Sunday as the Christian day of worship appears even within the New Testament. In one of his letters to the Corinthians, Paul advises the Church members at Corinth to put aside some money 'every Sunday' (or, more literally, 'on the first day of every week' — as in RSV) so that they will not require a special collection for the Church at Jerusalem when he arrives (1 Cor. 16.2). Elsewhere in the Corinthian correspondence, Paul reminds his readers that such contributions should be given freely and not reluctantly, for 'God loves a cheerful giver' (2 Cor. 9.7). Cheerfulness in giving is to be a mark of this day of joy. Again, the writer of the Apocalypse tells us that he was 'caught up by the Spirit' on the Lord's day (Rev. 1.10).

These references to Sunday in the New Testament can be paralleled by instances from the apostolic fathers. In the Letter of Barnabas, for example, the writer argues strongly for the Christian day of worship as the fulfilment of the Jewish Sabbath and concludes: 'Wherefore we also celebrate with gladness the eighth day in which Jesus also rose from the dead, and was made manifest, and ascended into heaven.' In the Didache, we find this exhortation: 'On the Lord's day of the Lord come together, break bread and hold Eucharist, after confessing your transgressions.'

The association of joy with the worship of the Church on the Lord's day is clearly seen in the writings of Tertullian at the beginning of the third century. He contrasts heathens, with their annual festive days, and Christians, for whom every eighth day was a festive day (*De Idolatria* 14). In particular, joy was a special characteristic of worship on Easter day and at Pentecost. While Tertullian argues that Christians should kneel before God for the very first prayer each day as well as in public worship, he states that kneeling is prohibited on Easter day and at Pentecost to emphasize the joy of worship at both these seasons (*De Oratione* 23).

Joy in worship was thus a marked characteristic of the early Christian Church. This joyful worship has its counterpart in heaven. The writer of the Book of Revelation describes the new song of the redeemed

(Rev. 5.9-10, 14.3, cf. 15.3-4). So 'the earliest Church, though she worshipped in very humble meeting-places, reached out her arms towards a fellowship that was world-wide and heaven-high; and the joy of her worship on earth was attuned to the majestical joy of the worship above.'[2] Similarly, in what has been called 'one of the purple passages of the New Testament',[3] the author of the Letter to the Hebrews contrasts the exultation of Christian life and worship with the gloom and fearfulness of life under the old covenant. When Christians worship God, it is to no sombre Sinai that they come. It is to the heights of heaven, where they join in the worship offered by angels and 'the spirits of good men made perfect' (see Heb. 12.18ff.).

Public Worship Today

All this has important implications for the present day. Joy should be an indispensable characteristic of Christian worship every Sunday of the year. The fact that many have lost this sense of joy in worship is one of the criticisms made of the Christian Church. Jesus Kids, for example, complain that members of an ordinary congregation show 'no spontaneity, no joy, no expression in their actions of worship which would indicate that God has done anything in their lives worth getting excited about'.[4] Their description of the modern Church at worship, caricature though it may be, is far different from the revitalized worship characteristic of the early Church in the first century A.D.

To many Christians, the ecstatic worship associated with the charismatic movement appears to be an over-emphasis of the sentimental or emotional aspect of religion to the detriment of a more sane and intellectual approach to worship. After all, we are expected

49

to love the Lord our God with the whole of our being. Nevertheless, the authentic note of Christian joy should surely be sounded in every service of worship. This can be achieved by more meaningful participation in worship by members of the congregation, by a better understanding of the function of the choir and organist as leaders of congregational praise, and by preaching that is both faithful to the biblical text and relevant to the spiritual needs of the worshippers. The emergence of new hymns and new tunes is no doubt part of the answer, though by no means the whole answer. Some modern hymns are attempts to reintroduce the note of joy into Christian worship.

This note is probably more in evidence on Easter Sunday, when we sing our hymns of the resurrection; but the very origin and essential meaning of the Lord's day call for triumphant rejoicing throughout the Christian year. Every Sunday should be a celebration of the resurrection of Jesus Christ from the dead and ought to have about it something of the joy of Easter. The dominant note of worship must be one of rejoicing. 'Do not let us belie the gospel by dreary, joyless worship: it is not so that it is endeared to ourselves or commended to others.'[5] 'If we have lost this note [of joy] — and who can deny that many of us have lost it? — it is through worship that we must recapture it.'[6]

Joy in Life

Christian joy is not confined to the first day of the week, however. It affects our daily life and work in the world as well as our public worship of God on Sundays. There is a place in our religion for joy in life as a whole as well as for joy in worship. 'Sunday is not separate from other days for the mere sake of separateness. It is separate in order that it may leaven all other days with its hallowing influence. Sunday is a failure unless it makes the whole week Christian.'[7]

Our supreme guide to joy is Jesus, since joy was an ever-present reality in his life and work. Wherever he went in Galilee, he left some mark of cheerfulness and hope in the lives of the common people. He travelled about the country 'in the midst of a continual feast', as Renan put it. 'His entering a house was considered a joy and a blessing.'[8]

Even though the joy of Jesus shines through the gospel records, there are only three passages in which the evangelists refer to his personal joy. In the first, Luke tells us that the 'exultant joy' of Jesus on the return of the seventy missionaries was inspired by the Holy Spirit (Luke 10.21). The other two passages are in the fourth Gospel (John 15.11, 17.13). In the course of the farewell discourses, we learn that the joy of Jesus was the joy of unbroken fellowship with his heavenly Father and of whole-hearted obedience to the Father's will.

Jesus kept emphasizing the need for a joyful attitude to life. He offered to those who had faith in him for-giveness for the past, help and comfort for the present, and hope for the future. He therefore greeted life with three cheers — for the past, the present, and the future.[9] To the paralytic man brought to him by four friends, he said: 'Cheer up! Your sins are forgiven' (Matt. 9.2 — my own translation). To the superstitious disciples, storm-tossed in their small boat on the Lake of Galilee, he gave a shout of assurance: 'Cheer up! It is I; do not be afraid' (Matt. 14.27 — my own trans-lation). Within the context of the farewell discourses, Jesus summoned his disciples to have peace and cour-age. 'Cheer up! The victory is mine; I have conquered the world' (John 16.33 — my own translation).

Christian joy is not something superficial that withers away at the least sign of trouble. The joy of Jesus was joy through the cross. Neither suffering nor death could quench his spirit. 'For the sake of the joy that lay ahead of him, Jesus endured the cross, making light of its disgrace', and now enjoys the reward for his sufferings in that he 'has taken his seat at the right hand of the throne of God' (Heb. 12.2). This paradox of joy in suffering runs through the whole of the New Testament and is an essential element in the Christian religion.

In spite of the fact that early Christians had often to undergo suffering and persecution, life for them was a festival, as Paul realized when writing to the Christians at Corinth. Since Christ has died for us, we are called upon to enjoy the Christian life as a festival — not with 'the old leaven, the leaven of corruption and wickedness, but only [with] the un-leavened bread which is sincerity and truth' (1 Cor. 5.8). Since our joy and confidence are founded upon what Christ has done for us in his death and resurrection, we are called to live lives of ethical purity and cheerful hope.

The metaphor of the festival of Christianity appears in other writers within the first four centuries of the Christian era. Chrysostom, for example, said: 'All life is a festival since the Son of God has redeemed you from death.' Similarly, Clement of Alexandria stated that the entire life of the perfect Christian who excelled ordinary believers was a sacred festival. While Clement limited the application of the metaphor to a few Christians who could practise mystical philosophy, Paul and Chrysostom used it of every believer who had been redeemed from sin by the death of Christ.

52

Joy in life is not the preserve of a select few, whether they be mystic philosophers, Pentecostalists, Jesus Kids, or any other group. It is — or should be — the common possession of all Christian people. 'We Christians must get the joy of Christ back into our religion. We are denying Christ by losing it.'[10]

6

WE LIVE FOR CHRIST

The Christian life is a life of service from beginning to end. We are called to love and to serve God and our fellow men for the sake of Jesus Christ. The parable of the sheep and the goats teaches us that whatever we do for others is done for Christ (Matt. 25.40).

Obedient love was given a central place in the ethical teaching of Jesus, as we see from the second half of the double commandment: 'Love the Lord your God... Love your neighbour as yourself' (Mark 12.29f. = Matt. 22.37-40 = Luke 10.27). Mark emphasizes the connection between belief in one God and obedience to this command. By integrating the command to neighbourly love with the parable of the good Samaritan, Luke emphasizes the insistence of Jesus upon service to those in need, irrespective of their creed or their nationality.[1]

Jesus himself found true happiness in such obedient love. He had dedicated himself to a life of service to all around him. He had not been born into this world to be served but to serve, and to make the supreme sacrifice of life itself for the sake of all mankind (Mark 10.45 = Matt. 20.28).

The fourth Gospel also emphasizes the lesson of joyful service taught by Jesus. In the upper room, after washing the feet of the disciples, Jesus declared that they must be prepared to serve one another as he had served them. Then follows the beatitude of service: 'If you know this, happy are you if you act upon it' (John 13.17). Such a moral interpretation of this enacted parable may be combined with a soteriological interpretation; for the whole motif of the passage is cleansing. Jesus said to Peter: 'If I do not wash you, you are not in fellowship with me' (John 13.8). Compare 1 John 1:7: 'We are being cleansed from every sin by the blood of Jesus his Son.' What the risen Christ is saying to us, therefore, through the enacted parable of the feet-washing is that those who have been cleansed from sin through his death on the cross are called to love and to serve others as he has loved and served us. The beatitude pronounced by Jesus on such ministry draws attention to the joy that comes to those who follow his example of self-forgetful love.

An earlier incident in the fourth Gospel — the sequel to Christ's discussion with the woman of Samaria beside Jacob's well at Sychar — also brings before us the joy of Jesus and his disciples in the prosecution of their spiritual work. In the greatly accelerated process of growth amongst the population of the Samaritan village, the word of God sown recently by Jesus in the heart of the Samaritan woman was now ready for harvesting by the disciples. Sower and reaper could rejoice together in this rapid response to their service for God at Sychar (John 4.36). The promised age of fulfilment, foretold by one of the Hebrew prophets (Amos 9.13), had now arrived.

Duty of Joy

There are two passages in New Testament letters in which the duty of joy in service is specifically expressed. The Christians at Rome are reminded by Paul that they should be cheerful in spirit whenever they are trying to help those in distress (Rom. 12.8). The last phrase in this verse is rendered by James Moffatt as, 'the sick visitor must be cheerful'. This is no doubt part of what Paul is saying here; but the Greek words have wider significance. The phrase includes such things as the helpful kindness shown by the good Samaritan to the man who fell among thieves (Luke 10.37). The parable of the sheep and the goats (Matt. 25.31-46) also enumerates 'acts of mercy' (Rom. 12. 8 – RSV) – giving food to the hungry, drink to the thirsty, hospitality to strangers, as well as visiting the sick and those in prison. These, and all other deeds of compassion, are to be done with cheerfulness. 'Whoever shows kindness to others must be cheerful about it too' (Rom. 12.8 – TT).

The author of the Letter to the Hebrews realized that Church leaders could find joy in service only when they received due respect and obedience from those under their charge. The task of caring leadership could be a happy experience if those being cared for were responsive (Heb. 13.17).

Apostolic Joy

The apostle Paul took great pride in the Churches which he had founded in various cities in Asia Minor and in Europe. He also rejoiced in those whom he could claim as his own converts to Christianity. He took particular delight in the Church at Thessalonica and felt grateful to God for all the joy he had experienced through his work among the Christians there (1 Thess. 3.9). He had even permitted himself to boast in other churches of their steadfastness and faith (2 Thess. 1.4).

In spite of the strained relations that developed at one point in Paul's dealings with the Church at Corinth, we find frequent mention of his joy and pride in that Church in the Corinthian correspondence. Towards the end of 1 Corinthians, the apostle emphasizes a point about the resurrection of the body, protesting by his 'pride' in the Christians at Corinth (1 Cor. 15.31). In 2 Corinthians — a letter of reconciliation written after the breach between the apostle and his readers had been healed — he insists upon his confidence and pride in the Corinthian Christians. His joy in them is only matched by their joy and pride in him (2 Cor. 1.14; 2.3; 7.4, 14).

The Christians at Philippi also provided Paul with this sense of joy in service. When he remembered his work among them, he could pray for them all with joy (Phil. 1.4). He asked them to complete his joy 'by thinking and feeling alike, with the same love for one another, the same turn of mind, and a common care for unity' (Phil. 2.2). This joy in service remained with the apostle even when his work for Christ appeared to be leading him to a martyr's death (Phil. 2.17).

In chapter sixteen of the Letter to the Romans, Paul rejoices over the obedience of certain Christian believers to whom he is writing (Rom. 16.19). The tone of this verse lends further strength to the view that chapter sixteen could not have been part of the letter as originally written to the Church at Rome and that it was added on to the first fifteen chapters when Paul sent the letter to Ephesus. Paul was not in the habit of rejoicing over a Church that he had never even visited. The previous chapter — which was undoubtedly part of the original letter to Rome — contains a general statement of Paul's joy in apostolic service: 'In the fellowship of Christ Jesus I have ground for pride in the service of God' (Rom. 15.17).

An eschatological element is introduced into Paul's

apostolic joy when he declares that, through the faithful witness and steadfast endurance of his converts in the Christian life, he will have reason to be proud in the day of Christ. They will be 'proof that I did not run my race in vain, or work in vain' (Phil. 2.16). At that great time, his loyal Christian converts, whether they be Philippians or Thessalonians, will be his joy and crown of boasting, clear proof that his work has been fruitful. The joy of the Christian in the service of Jesus Christ is something that can withstand the ravages of death. It will endure into the next world as a garland of victory (Phil. 4.1; 1 Thess. 2.19).

Some late manuscripts of the New Testament (those lying behind the *textus receptus* translated in the Authorized Version) insert the words 'with joy' into the narrative in Acts when Paul is making his farewell speech to the Ephesian elders: 'For myself, I set no store by life; I only want to finish the race *with joy*, and complete the task which the Lord Jesus assigned to me' (Acts 20.24). Even if these two words are not part of the authentic text of Acts, they express the true sentiment of Paul, as seen from various passages in his letters. 'The close of his life was to be no faint, trickling stream making its painful journey over the sand to the sea, but an ever-deepening, ever-widening river that brought to the ocean its own exulting fulness.'[2]

This joy in the service of Christ was shared by the apostle with those who worked with him. We get a glimpse of this in 2 Corinthians, where Paul tells his readers that, while he himself rejoiced because of the renewed confidence he now had in them, he was also 'delighted beyond everything by seeing how happy Titus is: you have all helped to set his mind completely at rest' (2 Cor. 7.13). It is possible that Titus had been to Corinth to try to heal the breach between the apostle and his Church. If so, the success of his mission had given him great joy — joy in service accomplished in the name of Jesus Christ and for the sake of the peace and unity of the Christian Church.

Complete Joy

The purpose of the author of 1 John in writing his letter was the completion of his joy as well as that of his readers (1 John 1.4). Those who have been entrusted with the word of God must share it with others before they can expect to have true Christian joy. This joy can grow only through service. It must find expression in this way in order to be fully possessed.

In his second letter (probably written by the same person) John the Elder expresses his hope of visiting 'the Lady chosen by God and her children' in the near future and of talking with them face to face. The object of John's proposed visit (probably to some particular congregation within the 'diocese' of Ephesus) is the same as that which the writer had in view in sending 1 John (probably to the whole 'diocese'), namely, 'that our joy may be complete' (2 John 12).

These passages from the Johannine Letters indicate that the reason for joy in Christian service is the realization of Christian fellowship, which is fellowship both with Christ and with one's fellow Christians. Since this fellowship (or 'communion') is created by the Holy Spirit, Paul can refer to it as 'fellowship in the Holy Spirit' (2 Cor. 13.14) or 'the fellowship of the Holy Spirit' (RSV) or 'the fellowship the Holy Spirit gives' (WmB).

The idea of fellowship with Christ in Christian service is given expression at the close of Matthew's

Gospel. The commission given to the disciples by the risen Christ before his ascension was accompanied by the promise of his continuing presence with them (Matt. 28.19f.).

So it turned out in practice. As the apostles went out on their mission to the world as Christ's witnesses, they were conscious of the fulfilment of his promise through the agency of the Holy Spirit. Inspired and strengthened by the divine presence, they went on their way with a newborn joy — a joy that fitted them for service and that grew by service.

So it has proved throughout the centuries. Countless Christians have experienced the joy of Christian service. They have been inspired by the presence of the risen Christ with them as they fulfilled his commission. We, too, can live for Christ and rejoice in his service.

7

WE DIE TO LIVE

In recent years, we have become familiar with the idea of realized eschatology. With the coming of Jesus Christ, the reign of God has broken into history and the purposes of God have been revealed as never before. The joy that accompanied the birth at Bethlehem was due to the fact that this baby in the manger was none other than the Messiah expected by the Jews, the Son of God sent into the world 'when the right time came' (Gal. 4.4 — TT). In his teaching, Jesus often struck this note of fulfilment. He was intensely conscious of the fact that in his own person and ministry the hopes of all the years had been realized.

While ancient Jewish eschatology was in large part fulfilled with the coming of Jesus Christ, Christianity has posited its own essential doctrine of the last things. Although the reign of God has already broken into history in the event of the incarnation, the Christian still looks forward to its fuller coming in this world or in the next or in both. Eschatology must always find a place in Christian theology, for 'religion without a great hope would be like an altar without a living flame'.[1]

For this reason, the phrase 'realized eschatology' has been emended to 'inaugurated eschatology'.[2] This new phrase takes account of Professor C.H. Dodd's great insight: that Jesus taught that something of great significance had happened with his coming into this world and with his proclamation of 'the gospel of God' (Mark 1.14). It also takes account of the future element in the teaching of Jesus. In the Synoptic Gospels, as in other parts of the New Testament, there is a paradoxical tension between the 'now' and the 'not yet'; for Jesus taught that the reign of God was already present in his own ministry and also that his disciples should pray for its extension on earth as in heaven (Matt. 6.10 = Luke 11.2). At the same time, there was an eschatological note in the teaching of Jesus. The reign of God would be realized in its fullness only 'when the Son of Man comes in his glory' (Matt. 25.31) and on the day when 'your Lord is to come' (Matt. 24.42). 'Keep awake then; for you never know the day or the hour' (Matt. 25.13).

While Christian eschatology, therefore, is not only realized but still to come (and so 'inaugurated'), there is a certain amount of dubiety among Christians as to what is really involved in this doctrine. As far as the New Testament is concerned, the main emphasis is on the second coming of Christ at the end of the present age, when all men will be judged by him. On the other hand, in popular usage eschatology is looked upon as dealing with the Christian hope in life after death — which is also found in the New Testament — and in this the concept of joy plays an important place. Our purpose in this chapter is to assess the relevance of both aspects of eschatology to the concept of joy, though the main emphasis will fall upon the extent to which the doctrine of the hereafter contributes to the joy of the Christian in the present world.

Beatitudes of Jesus

Eschatological joy played a large part in the teaching

of Jesus, as we can see from the beatitudes and from his parables. The eschatology of the beatitudes is both realized and futuristic. All the types of people mentioned in them (Matt. 5.3-12; Luke 6.20-3) — or the various facets of one type of person, the humble Christian believer — are happy here and now, partly because of the presence of the Messiah with them in the person of Jesus, partly because of the joy that will be theirs hereafter.

'The kingdom of heaven' is a present reality as well as a future hope for 'those who know that they are poor' (Matt. 5.3; cf, Luke 6.20) and for 'those who have suffered persecution for the cause of right' (Matt. 5.10). The promise of consolation to the sorrowful (Matt. 5.4) was partially fulfilled with the coming of Christ and with the mighty acts of God in the cross and the resurrection, but further fulfilment has still to come at the consummation of all things. The good things of the messianic kingdom are promised to 'those of a gentle spirit' (Matt. 5.5). Those who ardently desire to see right prevail will eventually see the victory of God (Matt. 5.6); those who show mercy can expect God's mercy on the day of judgement (Matt. 5.7). The beatific vision is for those whose hearts are pure — 'they shall see God' (Matt. 5.8). Peacemakers even now are called 'sons of God' in Christ, as Paul came to realize (Matt. 5.9; cf. Rom. 8.14), but hereafter they shall be able to claim their inheritance in full — 'God shall call them his sons' (Matt. 5.9).

While a certain anticipation of joy is hinted at as an experience in the present world, the beatitudes of Jesus, one and all, pass beyond this world for their final consummation and for the full happiness of Christ-like character. Yet the joyful rewards promised in the future world are only variations of the same theme. They are different ways of expressing the truth that those who follow the example of Christ can be assured of joy both now and hereafter. In this world, they can enjoy in anticipation the blessings of the future messianic kingdom. These blessings include the divine consolation at the consummation of all things, the vindication of right, and the mercy of God on the day of judgement. They also include the vision of God and the full realization of divine sonship in the world to come. The fact that such great rewards are awaiting Christians in heaven ought to make them able to rejoice here and now, no matter what persecutions and sufferings they may have to endure.

Parables of Jesus

The eschatological joy of the righteous is also emphasized by Jesus in some of his parables. In the parable of the talents, for example, the faithfulness of the first two servants is rewarded with the same commendation from their master, who shares with his faithful servants his own joy — the happiness of heaven and the bliss of the messianic meal (Matt. 25.21,23).[3]

Similarly, those placed at the right hand of the Son of Man in his glory at the last judgement are given possession of the kingdom that has been prepared for them since the beginning of the world (Matt. 25.34).

In both these parables, the wicked are punished, the slothful servant by being cast into outer darkness and those on the left hand of the King by being banished from his presence into eternal fire. Both punishments emphasize, by their contrast to the rewards, one of the chief elements in the joy of the righteous:

their association with God and with Christ in heaven.

Messianic Banquet

We have already noted one possible reference to the messianic meal in the reward given to the faithful servants by their master (Matt. 25.23). There may be another such reference in Luke's record of the table-talk of Jesus in the house of one of the Pharisees. Having noticed the number of distinguished citizens who had been invited to the meal, Jesus told his host that when he gave a dinner he should invite those who could not return the compliment. He added that such spontaneous generosity would bring him the pleasure of doing a kindness not to be repaid except 'on the day when good men rise from the dead' (Luke 14.14). If this refers to the messianic banquet, then the reward would be similar in kind to the dinner given to the poor on earth. In the teaching of the Pharisees, the happiness in store for the pious in the world to come was represented as a wonderful banquet and their chief joy consisted in being in the actual presence of God, an idea which is found in the Old Testament (Isa. 25.6).

The banquet motif appears in the account of the last supper Jesus shared with his disciples in the upper room of a house in Jerusalem. In handing over the cup, Jesus said: 'I tell you this: never again shall I drink from the fruit of the vine until that day when I drink it new in the kingdom of God' (Mark 14.25 = Matt. 26.29; cf. Luke 22.18). Matthew emphasizes the fact that the disciples will share the joy of the messianic meal by inserting the words 'with you' — '. . . until that day when I drink it new with you in the kingdom of my Father'.

Thus Jesus adopted this metaphor of the banquet, which appears frequently in Jewish literature, as a useful description of eschatological joy (cf. also Luke 14.15-24; 22.29, 30).

Fourth Gospel

There are several eschatological hints in the fourth Gospel. While the joy of John the Baptist, Abraham, and many others was fulfilled with the coming of Jesus Christ, the evangelist realized that the final fulfilment of Christian joy could come in its perfection only at some future time. The joy of unbroken fellowship with the Father and with the Son could be realized in its perfection only in the next world. Yet this eschatological joy could be experienced in anticipation by Christians in this world in so far as they obeyed the commands of Christ and received an answer to their prayers in his name (John 15.10f.; 16.24).

Furthermore, the whole concept of eternal life — a favourite Johannine motif — involves both aspects of eschatology, realized and futuristic. While the emphasis is placed upon life as the present possession of believers, the idea looks forward as well to the last day for its completion. The will of God is that everyone who trusts in Jesus Christ shall possess eternal life and be raised up on the last day (John 6.40). According to the fourth Gospel, Jesus took for granted the idea of a resurrection for both good and bad alike, a resurrection to life and a resurrection to judgement (John 5.29; cf. 11.23ff.).

Jesus never defined clearly the nature of the next life, but he indicated that its chief joy for the Christian would lie in his being in the company of Christ himself (John 12.26; 13.36). He promised his disciples that they would live with him in the Father's house of many rooms (John 14.3). Because he was going to the Father, he rebuked them for their sadness (John 14.28) and implied that they would eventually share in an intimate fellowship with himself and with the Father in the eternal world. Meanwhile, they could count on the promised gift of the Holy Spirit as a perpetual presence with them on earth (John 14.16).

The Apostle Paul

There are several important references to future joy in Paul's letters. The apostle links joy with Christian hope in his letter to the Romans. He expresses his own exultant hope and that of his readers as they look at their lives in the light of the divine splendour that is to be theirs (Rom. 5.2). Joyful boasting is by no means quenched by suffering, since hardship only increases the hope that Christians have on account of the presence of the Holy Spirit in their hearts. So Christians are exhorted to rejoice because of their hope (Rom. 12.12). They are reminded that this hope is a gift from God, who can fill them with joy and peace through their faith in him (Rom. 15.13).

But what is the nature of this Christian hope in which Paul can rejoice? The apostle defines it in the course of 2 Corinthians. He gives as his reason for always being of good courage his knowledge that 'so long as we are at home in the body we are exiles from the Lord', and he declares that he 'would rather leave our home in the body and go to live with the Lord' (2 Cor. 5.6,8). Although Paul seems to imply here that he cannot be with Christ while he is still alive, fellowship with the risen Christ played an important part in his personal religious life. Over and over again, we find him using Greek words compounded with the preposition *sun* (= with) in order to express his thoughts. Some of these words may well have been coined by himself. He seems to have felt 'the painful inadequacy of language to convey the unique "with-ness" that Christians have in Christ'.[4] In the following passage from the Letter to the Ephesians, there are no less than three such compound verbs: 'God. . . brought us to life *with* Christ. . . And in union *with* Christ Jesus he raised us up and enthroned us *with* him in the heavenly realms' (Eph. 2.4ff.; cf. Col. 2.13). In the Letter to the Romans, he maintains that even now we are 'heirs of God and fellow heirs *with* Christ, provided we suffer *with* him in order that we may also be glorified *with* him' (Rom. 8.17 — RSV).

It can thus be seen that union with Christ is the heart of Paul's religion. Nevertheless, as these passages imply, this experience looks beyond the present life to the future. Glorious though the experience may be here and now, it points forward to something still more wonderful to come: a richer, fuller fellowship in the next world. Although Paul could say that it was Christ who lived in him (Gal. 2.20), he could also say that 'to depart and be *with* Christ' will be 'far better' (Phil. 1.23), and he could look forward with keen anticipation to the time when he would 'always be *with* the Lord' (1 Thess. 4.17).

It is obvious that Paul, like other early Christians, expected the quick return of Jesus Christ at his second coming. Much of his eschatology is therefore directed towards the end of the age, when all things would find their consummation and when God's reign would be truly inaugurated. Paul felt that, on that great day, the converts he had made in the various churches would be his 'hope or joy or crown of pride' (1 Thess. 2.19; cf. 2.20; Phil. 4.1). The steadfastness of these Christians in the faith would make Paul feel proud that he had not run in vain nor worked in vain (Phil. 2.16). The joy of service thus has an eschatological aspect in it.

Other Writers

In the Pastoral Letters also, eschatology is directed towards 'the day of Christ'. Christians can look forward to the happy fulfilment of their hopes 'when the splendour of our great God and Saviour Christ Jesus will appear' (Tit. 2.13; cf. 1 Tim. 6.15).

The recipients of the Letter to the Hebrews had joyfully accepted the plundering of their property in a recent time of persecution because they knew that they 'possessed something better and more lasting' (Heb. 10.34f.). For them, eternal realities — for the moment unseen — were of far more importance than material possessions, which were merely temporal. They were reminded by the author that the knowledge of eschatological joy hereafter had also strengthened Jesus in his time of trial. It was 'for the sake of the joy that lay ahead of him' that 'he endured the cross, making light of its disgrace'. As a reward for such patient endurance of hardship on earth, he 'has taken his seat at the right hand of the throne of God' (Heb. 12.2).

Joy, suffering, and hope are again combined in 1 Peter. The happiness of the life to come for Christians is emphasized. Even in the midst of present sufferings, they can look forward with hope and joy to the glories of the future life. The reason for this eschatological hope and its nature are defined in the opening doxology. It is because of the resurrection of Jesus Christ from the dead that Christians have been given 'new birth into a living hope'; this hope is 'kept for you in heaven'. Christians can rejoice in it even though they may have to suffer various trials in the present world (1 Pet. 1.3-6). They can rest assured

69

that their joy will be triumphant 'when Christ's glory is revealed' on the day of judgement at the end of the age (1 Pet. 4.13).

The eschatological reward awaiting those who endure trial in the present life is also referred to by James. Here it is 'the gift of life promised to those who love God' (Jas. 1.12). With such joy coming to him hereafter, a man may be called happy here and now, even in the midst of his sufferings.

In the Book of Revelation, the eschatological joy appropriate to the final victory of good over evil is described. Heaven and its inhabitants are called upon to rejoice over the defeat of the devil and over the fall of the great city of the enemy, namely Rome itself, referred to as 'Babylon' (Rev. 12.12; 18.21). The second coming of Christ is mentioned as a call to Christian watchfulness and as a promise of joy to the faithful: 'Happy the man who stays awake' (Rev. 16.15).

The joys of the redeemed in heaven are described in various symbolic pictures. Having washed their robes, they have access to the tree of life that stands in the Garden of God (Rev. 2.7; cf. 22.14), they are given the crown of life (Rev. 2.10), they have white clothes to put on (Rev. 3.18; 7.9), and they rest from their labours (Rev. 14.13). Furthermore, they share in the celebrations on the wedding-day of the Lamb (Rev. 19.7-9). This is parallel to the messianic meal motif in the Gospels. Special provision is made for martyrs, whose lot in the next world is particularly happy. They share in 'the first resurrection' (Rev. 20.6) and so realize the full joys of the redeemed immediately without having to wait a thousand years.

Being with Christ

In such ways as these, the writers of the New Testament

attempt to describe the eschatology of joy. They employ various metaphors in order to emphasize the fact that joy can never be fully realized in the present world but must find its fulfilment in the hereafter, either at the second coming of Christ at the end of the age or at the death of the individual Christian. That the individual aspect cannot be ruled out completely is shown, *inter alia*, by the words of Jesus on the cross to the dying thief at his side: 'I tell you this; today you shall be with me in Paradise' (Luke 23.43).

This saying also points to the essential element in the whole eschatology of joy as found in the New Testament. The supreme joy of the Christian is experienced in being with Christ. While various metaphors are used to express what is really inexpressible in human terms — 'things beyond our seeing, things beyond our hearing, things beyond our imagining, all prepared by God for those who love him' (1 Cor. 2.9) — they can all be summed up in this phrase: 'being with Christ'. That is the important truth emphasized by the New Testament writers over and over again. The life to come is to be lived with God and with Jesus Christ. Perfect fellowship with the Father and with the Son in a life that is free from the restrictions and the disappointments of earthly life — that, according to the New Testament, is the joy that awaits the Christian in the next world. Death is simply a physical incident on the way to a fuller and more satisfying existence in the presence of God. We Christians die to live for ever the joyful life of eternity.

Resurrection of the Body

An important element in the eschatology of joy is the doctrine of the resurrection of the body. Only three passages in the New Testament speak of the resurrection of all people, bad as well as good. In the parable of the sheep and the goats, all the nations are gathered before the throne of the Son of Man in his glory, and they are judged by him according to their deeds on earth. While those on his left hand are sent away to eternal punishment, the righteous enter eternal life (Matt. 25.31-46). The fourth Gospel quotes Jesus as predicting that those who have done right will rise to life and those who have done wrong will rise in order to hear their doom (John 5.28f.). The Book of Revelation pictures the last judgement in similar terms: 'I could see the dead, great and small, standing before the throne' (Rev. 20.12).

Apart from these passages, the New Testament speaks only of a resurrection of believers, when they will be given spiritual bodies. This resurrection is quite different from the Greek doctrine of the immortality of the soul. According to this latter belief, immortality was a natural endowment of mankind, whereas in Christianity the resurrection of the body to eternal life is a gift of God. It emphasizes two main points: identity and continuity between this world and the next. Each individual Christian keeps his own identity in the future life, where the whole person will share in the joys and privileges of the perfect kingdom of God. The next world is a continuation of the present life of the Christian, but it will be a life that is free from the sufferings and the restrictions imposed upon us by our physical bodies. As Christians, we are destined to a resurrection of this body, but it will be a body like the body of Christ in glory. So personal identity will remain in that new life, which is the continuation and the fulfilment of the joys experienced here on earth.

The whole subject of the eschatology of joy raises the vexed question of the morality of any system of ethics which includes a doctrine of rewards. Many people object to such a doctrine on the ground that it is unethical to do good for the sake of future gain in the next world. We should be virtuous, such objectors say, for the sake of virtue and not for anything that we are going to get out of it either here or hereafter.

There is a certain amount of truth in such criticism. Christianity should not be treated as a kind of insurance policy. If any person is a Christian merely because he does not want to run the risk of the possible consequences of his misdeeds in a hypothetical future life — or on the day of judgement — then his religion is a poor thing. Nevertheless, Jesus never said to any person: 'Do this because you will get a reward hereafter'; but only: 'Do this, and you will live' (Luke 10.28) here and hereafter and enjoy the fruits of happiness both in this world and in the next. The reward of eternal life was promised by Jesus as a direct and natural consequence of a certain attitude towards himself called faith, which comprised belief plus action. 'In other words, the "rewards" attached to Christian conduct and character are not discontinuous with these but being of like quality have the appearance of springing out of them.' [5]

The nature of the rewards is such that they would not appeal to the earthly-minded. Only those who live 'in Christ' here and now could consider it a joy and a blessing to live 'with Christ' hereafter. The rewards held out by Christ to men are such as appeal only to the virtuous.

The idea of merit is ruled entirely out of the count. Even when we do all that is commanded of us, we have but done our duty and have no claim on God for recompense (Luke 17.10). The gift God gives to Christians is eternal life, which is life lived in communion with Jesus Christ, and this gift is given freely (Rom. 6.23). The joy of the redeemed in heaven is therefore the free gift of the grace of God, which none of us can claim to deserve. This is one of the major differences between Christianity and Judaism. In the latter, man earns his reward; while in Christianity the gift of eternal life is undeserved and unearned by human beings. It is given by the grace of God.

Furthermore, the reward is the same for all — the kingdom of God or eternal life or salvation — as the parable of the labourers in the vineyard emphasizes. The workmen hired at the eleventh hour were paid the same wages as those taken on early in the morning (Matt. 20.1-16). There is no selfishness involved in the doctrine of rewards. One man's gain is not another man's loss, since the reward can be obtained by any number of people and by everyone without exception.

Finally, as Bultmann has put it, 'Jesus' attitude is indeed paradoxical; he promises reward to those who are obedient without thought of reward.' [6] Eternal life can be won only by those who obey Christ absolutely without ulterior motives.

> Who seeks for heaven alone to save his soul
> May keep the path, but will not reach the goal;
> While he who walks in love may wander far,
> Yet God will bring him where the blessed are. [7]

Threshold of Great Joy

Eschatology thus plays an important part in the Christian concept of joy. We cannot ignore the hereafter if we are to give true meaning and purpose to the present life. The joys of the world to come cast their spell upon the life of the Christian here and now. The joy of the redeemed can be enjoyed partially in anticipation, especially within the fellowship of the Christian Church and in the sacrament of the Lord's Supper, which, all through the centuries, has been regarded as a foretaste of the heavenly feast of joy. This future joy should affect the everyday life of the Christian believer. It gives him new hope and confidence in the face of the hardships of earthly life. `

Maeterlinck said that Christians should always live as on the threshold of great joy. That could be taken as a summary of New Testament eschatology and as an indication of the relevance of such eschatology to the Christian concept of joy. Living on the threshold of great joy, the Christian can rejoice at all times in the sure and certain conviction that 'what is seen passes away; what is unseen is eternal' (2 Cor. 4.18); for we die in order to live (cf. John 11.25).

8

ETERNAL JOY

The concept of joy is firmly based in the New Testament. Joy is, therefore, an essential element in all true Christianity. As Christians, we joy in God — Father, Son, and Holy Spirit — and should give expression to our gladness both in worship and in everyday life and work.

There have been times in the history of Christianity when this quality has been specially in evidence. It was a very marked characteristic of the disciples of Jesus and of the early Christian Church. The note of joy has been recaptured throughout the Christian centuries when men and women have been set on fire by their enthusiasm for Jesus Christ as Lord and Master.

By way of conclusion, we look briefly at certain pictures from different periods in the story of our religion when joy has been particularly apparent. We begin with a scene from the Old Testament; for there is joy in Judaism at its best.

Joy in the Lord

The first incident is set in the city of Jerusalem in the year 397 B.C. Ezra has just returned from Babylonia with a new and enlarged edition of the Jewish Law. The public reading of this book has moved the people to tears, and they have been stirred to new enthusiasm, gladly promising obedience to God in accordance with the precepts contained in this new book of the Law. It is a day of great happiness and merriment because of the publication of God's Law. The keynote of the whole celebration is struck in the words of Ezra, the priest and scribe: 'This day is holy to the Lord your God; do not mourn or weep. . . . Let there be no sadness, for joy in the Lord is your strength' (Neh. 8.9f.). So Ezra reminded the people in Jerusalem that religion for them should be a thing of joy — joy in the Lord.

Wedding Guests

We pass over more than four hundred years. A new sect has been born within Judaism — a Judaism that has by now lost most of the joy that it ever had. Religion for the majority has become a thing of restraints and prohibitions, with little room left for the joy in the Jewish Law that had been evident in the time of Ezra. Through the efforts of the Pharisees and their scribes, regulation upon regulation has been accumulated round every provision of the Law of Moses in order that the common people may know exactly what to do and what not to do to keep within the letter of the law. Little freedom and still less joy in the service of God remain for the ordinary Jew.

In sharp contrast to this Pharisaic legalism, Jesus and his band of disciples have been working and moving about Galilee with a lightheartedness that has struck a fresh note in religion for most of their contemporaries.

The disciples of John the Baptist notice the difference. One day, they put a challenging question to Jesus: 'Why do we and the Pharisees fast, but your disciples do not?' In reply, Jesus likens his disciples to wedding guests: 'Can you expect the bridegroom's

77

friends to go mourning while the bridegroom is with them?' (Matt. 9.14f.). The disciples of Jesus are like the wedding party accompanying the bridegroom to the place where he is to be married to his bride. There is no place for gloom in such an atmosphere!

Festival of Joy

The scene changes to Asia Minor and to Greece. Within two or three decades of the death and resurrection of Jesus Christ, Paul is writing from Ephesus to the Christian Church that he has founded in the city of Corinth. He calls upon these Christians to observe the festival of their religion in a joyful attitude to the whole of life with sincerity and truth. Because these people living in a heathen city have been converted to Christianity, they can look upon their life and worship as a festival of joy. 'Let us enjoy life as a festival' (1 Cor. 5.8 — my own translation).

The same is true throughout the Roman Empire, wherever the gospel has been preached and its message has been believed. As Chrysostom was to put it in the fourth century: 'All life is a festival since the Son of God has redeemed you from death' (cf. *supra*, p.52). It is this characteristic of joy that impresses and finally conquers the old, pagan world that has grown so hard and bitter. 'A conquering, new-born joy awoke, and filled her life with day.'[1]

Clothes of Cheerfulness

In the second century A.D., cheerfulness remains the dominant note of the Christian communities in spite of the ever-increasing tide of hatred and persecution. *The Shepherd of Hermas* — an apocalyptic treatise written about A.D. 140 or 150 — contains the following exhortation:

Put away from yourself sadness, and do not afflict the Holy Spirit that dwells in you. For the Spirit of God that was given to this flesh endures neither sadness nor constraint. Therefore clothe yourself in cheerfulness, which has favour with God always, and is acceptable to him, and rejoice in it. For every cheerful man works good and thinks good and despises sadness; but the bad man is always committing sin.

The Lord's Merry Men

The twelfth century sees the recapture of the early Christian mood of joy by Francis of Assisi and his followers. As they travel barefoot through the towns of Italy, they love to call themselves *Ioculatores Domini* — 'the Lord's Merry Men'. Though ill-treated in many places, they are always full of joy. So they 'remind the world that the welfare of man, the peace of his heart, the joy of his life are neither in money, nor in strength, but in an upright and sincere will. Peace to men of goodwill.'[2]

Wilson of the Antarctic

Turning to the twentieth century, we can trace the outworkings of Christian joy in Edward Wilson of the Antarctic. His life-story shows the same qualities as did that of Francis of Assisi, of whom he was a profound admirer. The life and soul of the expedition to the South Pole, he was always cheerful, especially in times of distress and difficulty. He believed that there was no situation in human life, however apparently uncongenial, that could not be made into a thing of perfect joy.

Edward Wilson's optimism shines out in his last letter to his wife: 'I leave this life in absolute faith and happy belief that if God wishes you to wait long without me it will be to some good purpose. All is for the best to those who love God. . . All is well.'[3]

Joy in the Depth

In such pictures as these, we see the spirit of joy throughout the centuries. If it is less in evidence today — and this is the criticism made by many of traditional Church members at the present time — then it is something that we need to recapture in all kinds of ways; for optimism is the mood of the Christian faith. Joy in life and worship, joy in service and suffering, joy inspired by the Holy Spirit — this joy is what is needed before the Church and individual Christians can be seen to be truly alive and faithfully witnessing to their Lord and Master.

Such joy, as Paul Tillich realized so well, is not something emotional and superficial (and perhaps this is where some of the Church's critics go wrong themselves).

Eternal joy is not to be reached by living on the surface. . . The moment in which we reach the last depth of our lives is the moment in which we can experience the joy that has eternity within it, the hope that cannot be destroyed, and the truth on which life and death are built. For in the depth is truth; and in the depth is hope; and in the depth is joy.[4]

NOTES

INTRODUCTION

1. Matthew Arnold, 'Obermann Once More' in *Lyric, Dramatic, and Elegiac Poems.* Macmillan 1881.

CHAPTER 1

1. Vincent Taylor, *Forgiveness and Reconciliation.* Macmillan 1941.
2. T.W. Manson, *The Teaching of Jesus* (C.U.P. 1931), p.94.
3. W. Bousset, *Jesus*, tr. J.P. Trevelyan, ed. W.D. Morrison (Williams & Norgate 1906), p.116.

CHAPTER 2

1. Cf. Dom Gregory Dix, *Jew and Greek* (Dacre Press: A. & C. Black 1953), p.5.
2. G. Dalman, *The Words of Jesus* (T. & T. Clark 1909), p.269. Dalman's rejection of these passages, however, appears to me to rest on inadequate grounds.
3. See Vincent Taylor, *The Virgin Birth.* Oxford, Clarendon Press, 1920.
4. Ibid., p.34f.
5. A.M. Hunter, *The Work and Words of Jesus* (S.C.M. Press 1950), p.30.

CHAPTER 3

1. It is possible to date these events to A.D. 30 and Paul's conversion to A.D. 33. During his visit to Jerusalem three years afterwards (Gal. 1.18), Paul could have received part of the tradition from Peter and James.
2. C.F. Evans, *Resurrection and the New Testament* (S.C.M. Press 1970), p.62.

3. Cf. R.H. Fuller, *The Formation of the Resurrection Narratives* (S.P.C.K. 1972), p.171.
4. R.H. Fuller, op. cit., p.70.
5. See R.H. Fuller, op. cit., p.103.
6. W. Marxsen, *The Resurrection of Jesus of Nazareth* (S.C.M. Press 1970), p.21.
7. R.H. Fuller, op. cit., p.23.
8. N. Clark, *Interpreting the Resurrection* (S.C.M. Press 1967), p.98.
9. See C.H. Dodd, *The Apostolic Preaching and its Developments*. Hodder & Stoughton 1936.
10. A.M. Ramsey, *The Resurrection of Christ* (Collins Fontana 1961), p.34f.
11. A.M. Ramsey, op. cit., p.22f.

CHAPTER 4

1. Amos, Hosea, Micah, Isaiah of Jerusalem (author of Isa. 1 to 39).
2. A.M. Hunter, *Paul and his Predecessors*, rev. edn (S.C.M. Press 1961), p.93f.
3. A.M. Hunter, *Interpreting Paul's Gospel* (S.C.M. Press 1954), p.108.
4. I prefer to date Galatians to about A.D. 49, thus making it Paul's earliest letter, though some would give that honour to 1 Thessalonians and date Galatians to a few years later, between A.D. 53 and 56, during Paul's three-year stay at Ephesus.
5. Cf. H.B. Swete, *The Holy Spirit in the New Testament* (Macmillan 1909), p. 209f.

CHAPTER 5

1. A.B. Macdonald, *Christian Worship in the Primitive Church* (Edinburgh, T. & T. Clark, 1934), p.2f.
2. A.B. Macdonald, op. cit., p.39.
3. W. Neil, *The Epistle to the Hebrews* (S.C.M. Press 1955), p.130.
4. R.C. Palms, *The Jesus Kids* (S.C.M. Press 1972), p.57.
5. James Denney, *The Epistles to the Thessalonians* (Hodder & Stoughton 1902), p.220.
6. J.S. Stewart, *The Wind of the Spirit* (Hodder & Stoughton 1968), p.53.

7. J.W. Diggle, *Short Studies in Holiness* (Hodder & Stoughton 1900), p.13.
8. E. Renan, *The Life of Christ* (Trübner & Co. 1864), p.149.
9. See R.E. McIntyre, *The Ministry of the Word* (Nelson 1950), p.57.
10. Hendrik Kraemer, as quoted by J.S. Stewart, op. cit., p.54.

CHAPTER 6

1. See V.P. Furnish, *The Love Command in the New Testament*. S.C.M. Press 1973.
2. G.J. Jeffrey, 'The Way of Joy' (in *The Expository Times* LIX, 1947-8, p.73).

CHAPTER 7

1. Henry Van Dyke, *The Story of the Other Wise Man*. Harper & Bros. 1903.
2. See, for example, A.M. Hunter, *The Work and Words of Jesus*, rev. edn (S.C.M. Press 1973), p.94.
3. For the idea that there may be a reference here to the messianic meal, compare C.G. Montefiore, *The Synoptic Gospels* (Macmillan 1927), vol.2, p.320.
4. J.A.T. Robinson, *The Body* (S.C.M. Press 1952), p.63.
5. A. Scott, *New Testament Ethics* (C.U.P. 1930), p.53.
6. R. Bultmann, *Jesus and the Word*, tr. L. Pettibone and E. Huntress (Ivor Nicholson & Watson 1935), p.79.
7. Henry Van Dyke, *The Other Wise Man*, preface.

CHAPTER 8

1. Matthew Arnold, 'Obermann Once More'.
2. Paul Sabatier, *Life of St Francis of Assisi* (Hodder & Stoughton 1906), p.185.
3. G. Seaver, *Edward Wilson of the Antarctic* (John Murray 1933), p.294.
4. Paul Tillich, *The Shaking of the Foundations* (Pelican 1962), p.69f.

INDEX OF BIBLICAL REFERENCES

87